Daring t

Daring to be Different

Being a Faith Family in a Secular World

SARAH JOHNSON

Illustrations by Kathryn Lamb

DARTON·LONGMAN+TODD

First published in 2004 by
Darton, Longman and Todd Ltd
1 Spencer Court
140–142 Wandsworth High Street
London SW18 4JJ

ISBN 0 232 52398 3

A catalogue record for this book is available from the British Library.

Designed and produced by Sandie Boccacci
using QuarkXpress on a G5 PowerMac
Set in 12/15pt Bembo
Printed and bound in Great Britain by
The Cromwell Press, Trowbridge, Wiltshire

Contents

What would you give for a special gadget that turned the job of raising your children into a magical experience?

Goodness knows there are already enough items and services on offer to comfort the anxious parent or to make bringing up children

Introduction

easier. You can buy oodles of toys and electronic games that keep the kids quiet for hours, in specialist child-friendly shops equipped with televisions for them to watch while you shop, and microwave ovens so that the darlings don't have to wait for their dinner for more than two minutes.

We have family-friendly restaurants, super-markets and public loos. We can book family-friendly holidays of every description. (We can also go on holidays where the tour operators' proudest boast is that families are not in the least bit welcome.) Everyone, it appears, wants to help families to have fun, and especially to be seen to be doing so. Politicians of all parties promote taxation and benefits policies as helping 'The Family', thus invoking a shapeless entity that everyone can recognise when they see it, but which nobody can easily define in words.

And have you noticed how many private health clubs there are which claim to be wooing 'the family'? One might have a cute swimming pool designed to look like a giant bathtub. Another offers pony rides, another tennis coach-ing with a professional, climbing lessons, fencing and judo. Hours of family fun are guaranteed, well out of the view of those families who cannot afford the membership fees.

Our society has a tendency, whenever money allows, to solve parenting problems by removing the root of the problem: namely, the child. Busy working parents get through the summer by packing off the kids to football camp, tennis camp, adventure camp, assertiveness camp, fat camp, occasionally even plain ordinary camp.

The snag with all these helpful ideas for making life apparently easier for parents is that eventually you have to get on with the difficult task of being a family, and no family-friendly equipment can do that for you. A visit to a family-friendly theme park can never be more fun than the family making the trip. However many nappy-changing facilities are laid on, however imaginative the kids' menu, however thrilling the rides or swishy the wheels of the new £500 all-terrain baby-buggy, none of these things can prevent family rows, sulks or tantrums.

At some point the unfriendly family has to pile back into the family-friendly car and face each other on the journey home. The child glued to a small screen has to start interacting with other people one day, and the child away at tennis camp all summer still has to come back home and face his warring parents.

The world outside the gates of the family-friendly private leisure club is one where dangerous drugs are on the open market, where parents are too scared to let children walk to school alone, where only about 5 per cent of television programming is made with children's interests in mind even though children watch as much television as adults, and where more and more children's futures are decided in family courts as a result of family breakdown.

These are real problems for the family, and they can't be solved by making laws that require nappy changing units to be installed in public lavatories, by adding the name of this year's superhero to a breakfast cereal in order to get children to eat it, or by banning the promotion of other foods to discourage children from eating them. 'It takes a village to raise a child', but a Shopping Village is no substitute.

Early in my parenting history I was very sceptical of any kind of self-help book which promised to sort parents' problems out, and I still am, not because the advice in such books is bad – it is usually very good indeed – but because it is rarely very new. Nearly all childcare books recycle the same handful of basic rules, changing the emphasis here and tacking on a catchy gimmick there. The best advice on children is that which has been tried and tested for a few generations.

Even so it was with some astonishment that as the years rolled by I realised that the most powerful tool I had in my small armoury of weapons with which to protect my children was something which my husband and I shared, and which was probably the oldest set of self-help rules in the business – our ordinary, mainstream Christian faith.

I was born into a quietly practising Anglican family (our church's tradition is one of flower arranging and architecture rather than 'witnessing', and detests any public display of faith) and I married a Roman Catholic. This meant that neither of us belonged to any of the energetic younger churches.

Nor had either of us experienced any exciting, life-changing event which pushed us into placing our faith at the centre of our lives. We had not been the recipients of miraculous healing events or blinding flashes of light – it just gradually turned out that as our children increased in number, and grew older, we found ourselves turning more and more often to our faith for support, guidance and structure.

Instead of being baggage we wanted to jettison, our faith became our best tool for becoming a happy family. Time and time again we found something in it that illuminated a problem, clarified a puzzle or mended a hurt. Something of the same kind might also have happened if we belonged to one of the other major world faiths, but as it happened we belonged to the Christian one.

More than one child in every three born in the United Kingdom is brought to a Christian church for the rite of baptism before the age of one. Most of those children probably never see the inside of a church again; others come from families which are already committed Christians and will be brought in regularly.

There is a third group of children whose parents, while the holy water is being poured over the baby's head, find a curious thought running through their own heads: 'This is a good feeling. Could we get into doing this regularly? Would there anything in this faith for us?'

It is for that group of thoughtful, open-minded parents that I wrote this book. I want to convey to you some idea of how supportive spirituality can be for you and your family as you grow together through the years.

I suspect many of those parents, standing proudly and hoping that the priest is not going to drop the baby, will feel that faith is not for them because it seems too much against the grain of modern life. Being a Christian does not look easy these days; the received wisdom is that religion is effectively dead and has nothing more to offer us. Because of the decline in church attendance, it is assumed that belief is dead, too, and that its adherents must be an insignificant minority.

Yet at least half the people in this country say that they not only believe in God but also in Christianity as a force. Seventy-one per cent of British people described themselves as Christians in the last national census. Seventy-one per cent is an unusual size for an insignificant, ignorable minority.

What I am seeking to do is to set out some ways in which having faith can enrich your family life and the way you interact with your children — and to describe the way it adds magic to the subtle art of bringing up a family. 'Christianity is a mistake', pronounces Philip Pullman, one of our leading children's authors, at the climax of his trilogy, *His Dark Materials*. I would like to counteract that view.

We shall meet some Christian families whose refreshing

normality and intelligence suggest that they are not people who go around making 'mistakes' or following daft superstitions. We shall look at how faith can help us to reassess our families and the way we communicate with each other, and most of all how it can positively shape our parenting style.

This is not the place for a major *apologia* for Christianity or for faith in general. There are many excellent and eloquent voices who do that supremely well and there is no point in my trying to compete with them. I would like instead to put at rest some of the myths and misunderstandings about the way what I call 'faith families' live, and offer some of their solutions for living.

For example, prayer is one of the most common features of any religion yet it is also highly mysterious and, to my mind, deeply misunderstood. Not many Christians I know have been taught how to do it well. So I would like to pass on some tips from families who have built prayer into their daily routine and find it a source of strength, and also to look at the misconceptions our children pick up about prayer.

Anyone who has looked after children for any length of time knows that clear and regular routines are very important. Young children, especially, need the familiar safeness of a daily structure – the security of the unshakeable bedtime is the foundation of many a happy childhood. I have found that faith families are on the whole unusually good at giving their children this kind of happy structure in their lives. They build faith into their meal-times, into their holidays and household chores, and use it as a way of adding a touch of magic to grey days.

We shall also look at some ways faith families stick together by imposing their own home-made traditions, rules and habits on themselves. Living with a tradition can be surprisingly exciting; inventing your own traditions is highly empowering. Every family can build its own traditions, if the family members are prepared to stick with them. But faith families also have the opportunity to tap into the complex, many-hued structure of the Christian year to give shape to their lives. The Christian year has been two thousand years in the making. You could call it the ultimate time-management tool. It is also the ideal teaching tool – the whole faith is laid out in bite-sized chunks, as the Christian year rolls around.

Our culture recognises far fewer seasonal changes than our ancestors did. Here in the United Kingdom, every infant-school child dutifully paints pictures illustrating the change of the seasons with the obligatory daffodils, beach scene, autumn leaves and snowmen, but the truth is that the rhythm of our lives remains more or less the same throughout the year; we start work at the same hour, eat the same food, watch the same television, in winter and summer – all we do to mark the seasons is to put on slightly different clothes to go outside.

To show how faith can help your family to rediscover the earth's seasons, we shall follow the Christian year from Advent (the weeks before Christmas) through to Pentecost, in the summer. Taking a cue from the Last Supper, we shall look at faith as part of daily mealtimes. Pentecost also brings thoughts of the Holy Spirit making direct and personal contact with Jesus' early followers, so I have used it as the starting-point for thoughts about children's own spiritual experiences, particularly through the rich imaginative world of children's books. We shall look at the way in which different aspects of our family and emotional lives come to the fore at different times of the year, and at how media and consumer pressures affect our families in the light of faith.

Many young families are rediscovering the companionship that comes from going to a church regularly. At its most practical, a church is a free, friendly, local resource where you can be fairly sure of running into someone with the same life problems as your own. Any mother of young children knows that it is practically impossible to know too many other mothers of young children, especially if you are at home with a baby on your own for the first time in your life. Making friends with other parents provides support, advice, shared knowledge, shoulders to cry on and someone to have a laugh with.

A religion adds up to far more than just a place of worship, however, and you won't learn much from one visit – too many people give up on faith after a couple of disappointing trips to a local church. Churches now make a real effort to make young families welcome, but the idea of turning up on a Sunday morning still seems bizarre to many parents who would rather have a lie-in. So I have gathered some advice from battle-weary parents on happy churchgoing.

In the past thirty years, the general debate on morality has seen a curious change. The mainstream, established religions such as Christianity and Judaism seem to have been gently pushed to the side, eased to the edge of the path labelled 'kooky'. Attitudes to Islam have changed even more violently and alarmingly. At the same interest in spiritualism, reincarnation, Feng Shui and even fortune-telling techniques such as astrology and Tarot cards have grown and grown. Astrology in particular has moved from being the preserve of the poor, frightened or sad to being a key topic of conversation among young people. 'What's your sign?' is now a respectable way of opening a conversation.

With the possible exception of reincarnation, not one of these alternative beliefs has a moral core. Astrology is based on the belief that the earth's position at the time of birth affects character. Tarot is based on the belief that some outer power alters the way cards with pictures on them fall in order to send the user a message. Feng Shui is based on a set of beliefs which include the idea that your furniture, incorrectly placed, drains energy from your home and your soul.

I know people who pay good money for advice in these skills, yet if I adhere to a set of beliefs which have weathered the test of thousands of years, been subscribed to by billions of people, which have instigated the foundation of millions of charitable works and institutions, inspired great art and, most importantly, which have embedded into our moral fibre concepts which we cannot imagine being without, I am told I am 'superstitious'.

The public image of Christians, especially of Christian parents, is not an impressive one, based as it is so heavily on myth and prejudice. When I mused that a possible title for this book might be *Do Christians Make Better Parents?*, a friend instantly quipped back, 'Wouldn't a better title be *Why Don't Christians Make Better Parents?*'

It was a good point – parents with faith, Christian or otherwise, do not necessarily make better parents than anyone else. But faith, spirituality and an open mind must surely be among the best tools there are for being the best parents we can be. It is up to us how we use them.

'... excepting, maybe, the hangovers.'

1

'Truly I tell you, unless you change and become like children, you will never enter the kingdom of heaven. Whoever becomes humble like this child is the greatest in the kingdom of heaven. Whoever welcomes one such child in my name welcomes me.'

(Matthew 18:3–5)

Families with Faith

Around the time of the birth of your child, there was a moment which defined your new life as a parent. It might have hit you there in the labour ward amid the medical paraphernalia, mess and confusion. It might have been months earlier, when you went shopping for baby clothes for the first time, or later, when you were left alone in peace at last, holding your child in your arms.

For some parents this special moment arrives as a flash of blinding light, for others as a warm glow. For some it is a sense of awe in the presence of new life, for others, a surge of pride at the realisation that this new person is theirs to look after, to protect, to love. For many of us the moment may even be tinged with fear as the enormity of the task ahead is glimpsed for the first time – and whether this be the first child, or the fifth, sixth or seventh in the family, the moment still retains an element of surprise. And that moment is best defined by the words: *This is my child, whom I love.*

This is the moment which new parents are referring to when they say that 'everything has changed for ever'. In that moment the whole world seemed to have shifted its priorities, altered its context. The future, too, seemed suddenly tremendously important because it belonged to this new, beloved little person. The world even looked different. Even the colours of the trees and buildings outside the hospital window seemed different, as though a magic spell had been cast over the whole scene, or a veil withdrawn to reveal deeper, brighter hues. Not everyone feels this way after childbirth, I admit, but surprisingly many do.

But we don't believe in magic. Or do we?

In real life, love plays the role which magic plays in children's stories: it transfigures. When we are children, love makes us believe that our Mum is the most beautiful, strongest, wisest Mum in all the world. As teenagers, we find love turning the dull morning journey to school into an epic of suspense – will *he* be on the bus this morning to see me with my new hairstyle? Was that text message as witty as I thought it was, or will *she* think I am only a pest? By lunchtime, will I be in heaven, or in hell?

Love turns a boring morning in a half-deserted city playground into an hour of joy and laughter as a young mother larks with her two-year-old on the swings or sees her three-year-old turn the pedals on the tricycle for the first time. Love turns a trudge round the supermarket into a groundbreaking expedition, as a five-year-old excitedly discovers he can read the letters and numbers on the shelves all by himself and his mum or dad is almost more excited about the discovery than the child is.

Christians believe in the transforming, transfiguring power of love as a force in the world. We believe that the extraordinary story of Christ, who by preaching for three short years and suffering a violent death, transformed the way men and women think about love and truth, contains a message of intense and infinite love for the world from its Creator.

So even if you are not a Christian, even if you don't believe in God, the truth is that when you become a parent and experience that awareness of the transfiguring power of love, you come nearer to the spirit of Christianity than at any other time of your life.

As a Christian I have found my faith completely transformed by the experience of having children. I was always the sort of person who wanted to be a Christian, at least to be a person of faith. But my faith was weedy and querulous. Becoming a parent forced me to think about the nature of humanity, the nature of self-sacrifice and its role in a civilised world, and to look again at the Gospels.

Many young parents who formerly never considered themselves to be in the least bit religious begin to go to church when their children are small. Their reasons for doing so, at a time when religion of any kind is pushed to the margins of public life, are fascinating.

Some of them may be what has been wittily termed 'eduChristians'. In Britain, church attendance can be a major factor in winning one's child a place at one of the many church-affiliated state schools; these are often regarded with more respect than the secular schools and places can be heavily over-subscribed. So there is a certain type of young family which appears for the first time in churches in around September, shaking hands enthusiastically with the vicar or priest: they need the vicar's recommendation on their school application form. Numbers thin out in February, after the local schools have made their choices.

Is this cynical? I don't think so. For some of those families, what begins as a pragmatic duty rapidly becomes a habit. They look around and notice that there are other young families like themselves in church and their prejudices against religion begin to crumble. Their children make friends in the crèche; the Sunday morning routine begins to be built around church. The parents begin to listen to what they are hearing from the pulpit. They find that the words of the Gospels are more challenging, more surprising and less bland than they had expected.

When I had my first baby, the stark, simple and profoundly humbling statements in the quotation at the beginning of this chapter jumped out at me with a force I had not noticed before.

The words *become like children* are doubly shocking when you are changing nappies. Your child lies on his back, wriggling his legs. He trusts you absolutely and has complete faith in you. So is this what Jesus wants us to become? I found myself for the first time feeling quite excited about the radical agenda, the outrageously non-conforming adventure that Jesus had set out for his followers.

So from being a rather limp and occasional effort at vague spirituality, my faith started growing muscles. It is still not exactly an Arnold Schwarzenegger among faiths. But instead of being a nagging burden – 'I really ought to be thinking about being a Christian' – it sometimes sweeps me along. Instead of being one of the most-often postponed items on the To Do list, my faith sometimes contrives to peer over my shoulder, seize the pencil and write out the To Do list for me, directing my priorities.

If the idea of a new sense of spirituality being connected with your experience of becoming a parent rings a bell, then this book may be for you. You may be considering returning to the faith you were brought up in, just to see if it had anything to offer. You may have been brought up in no faith at all yet are curious as to what Christianity might give you. Either way, you are ready to give faith a chance, and particularly to allow it to infiltrate your relationship with your child or children.

Most British homes are completely 'unchurched', even though most people have a vague idea that they belong to a faith of some kind. A large, very vociferous and powerful body of opinion believes we are better off without religion altogether. Religion is seen as retrograde, divisive and repressive. Since even most Christian families are not particularly good at discussing religious feeling at home, and since religion is rarely mentioned in the news except as a cause of friction or a wellspring of scandal, it is not surprising that religious experience is regarded as something the happy British home can well do without.

But my family and I have found the exact opposite. Our faith gives us so many advantages in the struggle to bring up our children happily, that I don't know how I would manage without it.

Of course we quarrel (constantly) and we have our problems in the past and no doubt waiting for us in the future. But I have found that having a faith has given us over the years:

+ **A structure to our daily life:** the discipline of attending church, the rhythm of the church year, the habit of daily prayers and saying grace at meals as often as we can manage. In a world of all-year-round (albeit tasteless) strawberries and everlasting 'classic repeats' on cable or digital television, it is comforting to know that certain things are done according to their season and are not moveable feasts.

+ **A way through problems:** praying, especially praying together, almost always seems to calm everyone down and opens doors to solving conflict. There is an American Evangelical group which works under the slogan 'What Would Jesus Do?' and it is not such a bad question, we have found.

+ **A solid basis for our moral viewpoint:** referring to Jesus' words, or the teachings of the Church, helps to ground us with rules. Even if some of us disagree with some of the rules, we at least have a starting-point for argument. 'It's because it would make God unhappy,' is the answer which our youngest child, when four, used to offer as a knock-down riposte to any moral question. We have to move on from this point – why would it make God unhappy? Why would this particular action be opposed to Jesus' teaching? – but it is a good start.

+ **A door to deep questions of spirituality and the unknown:** because we are living in daily awareness of our spiritual side, we probably have more discussion of the big questions in life than we might otherwise have. It is not a great, closed book to us, or an embarrassing area which we avoid. On the contrary, my family seems to feel more comfortable discussing the Infinite than discussing homework or money.

+ **The support of a community,** both on a personal level

and in a wider sense. We live in the middle of a huge and notoriously impersonal city. The knowledge that we have a 'village' in the form of our church community is greatly re-assuring. It enabled us to find a community of our own after moving from one district to another; being part of a church has enabled many faith families to find a community after moving from one country to another.

✦ **A sense of self-worth:** it confers the feeling that nothing we do is trivial – everything we do, every day, *matters*, and every moment of our lives here is precious.

✦ **The sense of 'losing our lives':** One of the scarier, most radical teachings of Jesus is the instruction to 'lose our lives' to God. We don't manage to do this very much. But in the moments when I try, when I contemplate turning everything over to God and try to become purely an instrument of his will, the sense of a burden lifted is intense.

Some Christian families

If you weren't brought up in a Christian home yourself, you might have somewhat hair-raising ideas about what a Christian home looks like. When did you last see a positive representation of a Christian family? According to popular British television, Christian parents are repressive, self-righteous, hypocritical, self-delusional and cruel. They are always fanatical and can be relied on to forbid their children from doing anything remotely enjoyable.

If a Christian, especially an Evangelical or a devout Catholic, pops up in a detective series, then you may consider it a 9–1 chance that he or she will turn out to be the murderer. According to the television universe, Christians beat their children routinely, forbid them from seeing other children whom the parents believe to be sinful, and are complete hypocrites who probably engage in sado-masochistic sex in private. Protestant vicars are always comically effete, with frustrated (and, surprisingly often, alcoholic) wives; Catholic priests are portrayed routinely as perverts, madmen or idiots.

Your chief source of information about American Christians may well be the irritatingly cheery next-door-neighbour Ned Flanders of the long running cult cartoon series, *The Simpsons*. One particularly clever episode focuses on Ned's inability to use strong language or lose his temper: he becomes fully human only after suffering, like Job, a series of terrible misfortunes. These teach him to express fallibility and doubt.

Real Christian homes are not like any of these – not usually, anyway. Christian parents have messy homes, cheeky youngsters, surly teens, missed deadlines, ill-advised credit card sprees, lost dinner money and Monday morning hangovers like the rest of us. But those who allow their faith to come out of church and right into their home invariably find that it gives them unbelievable strength in dealing with the ordinary crises and problems which life throws at us (excepting, maybe, the hangovers).

Karen (I have changed her name) is typical of modern British Christians. A highly intelligent, highly educated mother of two married to a scientist, she has 'church tasted' by visiting a range of churches in her area of North London, settling finally with the Church of England. 'Church tasting' is the typical way in which modern Christians find their way; rather than doggedly following in their parents' footsteps, it is becoming more usual for couples to shop around for faith.

In fact Karen has come to her faith not through tradition or the way of life handed down from her parents but by the opposite route: as a gentle reaction, a genteel form of rebellion, to her liberal, atheist intellectual upbringing.

Her home spills over with books and writing projects; the creativity of her son and daughter are much in evidence all over the house, with bits of handiwork and paintings stuck up all over walls. The children go to a church school, which takes a large proportion of children from other faiths, especially from

Islamic families. Karen's family attends church regularly, which observance places them in a small minority at the school – even though it is nominally a 'church' school.

Karen and her family do not evangelise in any formal or organised way. But the parents of their children's strict Muslim friends are – Karen has noted – more comfortable with the notion of their children being friends with churchgoing Christian children, than with the idea of them spending a lot of time with children from totally non-religious families. There is an unspoken bond between believers of any kind.

Another Christian parent who arrived from another faith is Ram Gidoomal, the Asian businessman who is also the chairman of the first religious political party to be formed in Britain, the Christian People's Alliance. Ram is far more up front with his Christianity: it is his job. A former Hindu, he came to be what he prefers to call 'a follower of Jesus' over a period of years: his parents were initially devastated by his choice. For them, and for many people of other faiths, especially in Asia, the word 'Christian' was not a description of a faith at all but a catch-all term describing the whole of Western culture with all its excesses and horrors. For Ram's parents, the words 'Christian culture' conjured up less the *St Matthew Passion* or Italian Renaissance painting than English football hooligans fighting and vomiting in the streets.

So Ram and his wife, Sunitra, created their own Christianity from scratch and gravitated towards the less mystical, more politically active Evangelical churches. For Christianity is a very diverse thing.

Its diversity is a strength, but it is not seen as such. 'Happy-clappy, born-again Christians have totally hijacked Christianity, so that people just think of organic hippies with open-toed sandals,' a young Catholic mother complained to journalist Anna Blundy in an article looking at the new generation of church-going young parents (*The Times Magazine*, 16 March 2002). This mother is annoyed because certain Christians routinely refer to themselves simply as Christians, rather than calling themselves Anglicans, Evangelicals, Methodists or whatever. The tentative Christian has a tricky first hurdle to overcome: and it is erected by the Christians themselves — it is the 'denominations' game. There is no Trades Descriptions Act in Christendom. No church is required to spell out on the sign outside the door just what its particular 'flavour' of belief or worship style is.

Such signs would be tremendously useful ...

The vicar here is a former Army Chaplain and we have a tremendous display on Remembrance Sunday. We don't do more than nod at each other in an embarrassed way at the Sign of Peace. Average age of congregation 63.

The priest in this Catholic church is an old CND campaigner — we ignore Remembrance Sunday completely. Expect guitars at the family service and a lot of fasting.

This City church is managed largely by its ambitious musical director for the benefit of bankers and lawyers who rarely attend it voluntarily in life, but all seem to require splendid memorial services as soon as they are dead. Don't bring toddlers or babies in — the semi-professional choir costs us a fortune and they do not take kindly to interruptions.

This village church is run by one quarter of a vicar who only comes down our way once a month. If you believe in God, please sign the flower arranging rota. If you want spiritual comfort, the doctor's surgery is open from 9:00 a.m. to 12.00 p.m. on weekdays.

Christians themselves, happily, refuse to fall into the neatly laid out categories which the press lay out for them. Journalists try hard to fit all Christians along a spectrum ranging from 'left' to 'right' in the same way they categorise politicians: it does not work.

Profiling the leading candidate for the top job in the Anglican church recently, one journalist noted with approval that he was 'liberal' on the subject of allowing homosexuals to become Anglican priests, but added with bemusement that he was also pro-life, as though the two stances were somehow incompatible. Even though Christians have given the secular world the basic building blocks of morality on which democracy stands – fairness, the principal of the strong protecting the weak, rights of the individual and so on – the secular world is still puzzled by the way people of faith do things.

Take Diana and her family. They are Roman Catholics; but they consider themselves as part of a loose grouping within the Catholic Church called the Catholic Charismatic Renewal which seeks to lay more emphasis on the work of the Holy Spirit than most Catholics do. This means that they join group prayer sessions which encourage profound meditation and speaking in tongues (a kind of ecstasy). They attend an ordinary Roman Catholic church, but one where the priest is also part of this loose grouping.

Diana's brand of Christianity sometimes extends to inviting homeless people and tramps into their home for meals ('we are told to welcome sinners: so we do – no harm has come to us through it yet'). They do this spontaneously and through a desire to answer Jesus' call to treat all men and women as brothers and sisters.

Many of the people Diana invites into her home are alcoholics, thieves and drug addicts: not the best examples to be offered to Diana's children. Diana's interpretation of her faith could not be more different from that of another Catholic mother, Helen.

Helen and her husband Kevin are Americans living in England. The couple, in their mid-thirties, moved to London partly to distance themselves from relatives in the United States whose lifestyle they felt set a bad example to their children. They felt this because one of their own siblings was cohabiting with a partner outside marriage. To get their children away from this influence, they moved across the Atlantic Ocean.

Kevin and Helen believe very firmly that the Tridentine (Latin) Mass is the only truly valid form of worship; they believe quite literally that the exact form of words used in the Mass is what makes it *what it is*: in other words, they believe that by changing the words of the Mass, even slightly, the Church takes away its power to turn the wafers and wine into Jesus' body and blood.

Helen believes that the Mass is a set form of words handed directly from God: 'This is the most important thing to happen in the universe,' she says. She reserves her most heartfelt prayer, that no untimely harm will come to those she loves, for the moment in the Mass when Jesus is believed to be bodily present among His people, in the belief that prayers are most likely to be answered if uttered at this point.

When you walk into Helen's home the first thing you notice is the holy water by the door waiting for family and visitors to use in making the sign of the cross. The next thing you notice is that the few ornaments and pictures are almost without exception religious in nature. There is a television and all the normal luxuries of a middle class life, but no fripperies. There is not a hint of sauciness or fun in the home; no display of any frivolously sexual nature, indeed no pictures that are not specifically religious, seem to be allowed.

Helen and Kevin are bringing up their children in the heart of their clear-cut style of faith. They are tough, but they have courage in holding to their convictions. This is admirable. Not many people manage to do this. Also admirable is the fact that the important decisions of their lives have been built on their beliefs, rather than the other way around: many self-styled Christians prefer to tailor their beliefs to fit with life choices that happen to be more convenient to them.

Helen says the Rosary on a regular basis with a group of friends and the family has a carefully planned prayer and devotion schedule. They have an unshakeable belief in the power of prayer that is enviable and a self-discipline that is admirable. But with it goes a certain inflexibility, perhaps even a lack of charity towards those of weaker will.

Even though they too have an unshakeable, fundamental type of faith, Greg and Agghi Clovis come across as a very different couple, with a very different atmosphere in their home from that of Kevin and Helen. This may have a lot to do with the fact that instead of two little toddlers, Greg and Agghi have ten children, the oldest being in their early twenties and the youngest a baby.

The couple are very strictly observant Roman Catholics, and when I asked if they planned to have more children, Greg politely answered: 'I wouldn't like to say.' From which I assume that the couple do not even use the natural methods of fertility control which are approved by the Vatican but prefer nature to take its course.

Greg, who works as the director of a pro-life pressure group, is a St Lucian by birth and Agghi an Iranian, so – a little like the Gidoomals – they have had to create and forge their own brand of Christianity without reference to an easily accessible, ready-made community. As a couple they are vital, warm, combative, frank and delightfully unpompous. Contrary to secular convention, there is an unmistakeable sexiness about parents of large families. A suburban house where a baby buggies, bikes and motorbike leathers jostle in the hall and baby's cries punctuate the night sends out the message: this couple still delight in each other and have been doing so for a long time.

The Clovises listen to their children, argue with them and relish the constant near-chaos of a large family. Their small army of teenagers have a clear set of rules about being out late, coming home for dinner and so on, which are enforced with no-nonsense sanctions. They are encouraged to think of themselves as a team, with a strict housework rota drawn up – and enforced – by Agghi.

If you want one expression to sum up the Clovis household, it would be: 'full of life'. The parents, who pepper their conversation with their children with references to God, to Christ and to God's will, seem powerfully aware of the importance of everything, but this awareness, far from casting a grave pall over the family, instead fills it with a sense of joy.

There are not very many families quite like the Clovises in Britain, but there are more like Charlotte's. Charlotte is an Anglican, a top health administrator and a woman of great personal faith: she is married to Mark, a writer and journalist who does not share her faith. They are part of an old-school English upper class, a section of society which is in many ways most hostile to any but the most superficial kind of faith. Charlotte often finds herself at odds with her peers and colleagues and is aware that as a Christian she is 'the odd one out'.

In contrast with Helen and Kevin's uncompromising avoidance of anyone whom they fear might be a bad influence on their children, Charlotte has had to learn to temper her faith with tolerance of the secular world; otherwise she could risk losing her friends and even jeopardising her marriage. Yet it was her agnostic husband who read Bible stories to her three daughters when they were tiny: it was he who urged her to lead a Lent prayer group; and the three daughters, now in their late teens, do not reject their mother's faith but accept it as something worthy of respect. They are not 'God-squadders' but they are thoughtful girls with a sense of spirituality. Charlotte is feeling now that her years of being 'the odd one out' are paying off at last.

What is it like to believe in God in Britain now? Anna Blundy, whom I quoted above, had recently started going to church when she wrote:

Going to church does make a lot of people feel better in a
lot of different ways. If it is just a question of enjoying the
lovely music ... of sitting in a beautiful building thinking
quietly for an hour, of listening to a thoughtful speech that
isn't being made for motives of political ambition or money,
of saying reassuringly familiar prayers and singing childhood hymns, or even of entertaining the possibility that
maybe ...

'... that maybe ...' – there is a God, of course. Blundy dares
not say the words for fear of being laughed at, for whereas it is
fashionable to talk of 'spirituality' it is not fashionable to believe
in God. Unfortunately such ambiguity just won't wash with
children. They don't buy vague, fence-sitting types of spirituality.
They want clear answers. 'Is there a God or is there not a God?'
they are inclined to ask. 'What happens when we die?', 'Are we
different from animals?' Once your children are old enough to
ask questions, they do so with forthright clarity. They want
answers, and they want them now.

Most of us are totally unequipped to answer the questions on
our own and find ourselves falling back on dimly-remembered
religious education lessons for support. This may very well mean
a simple, colouring-book spirituality or a quick bus-tour of the
superficial elements of World Faiths. Many people, digging out
their dusty memories of school spirituality, suppose that it is all
there is to be discovered about the subject, and reject the whole
subject as infantile. This is a little like a teenager losing interest in
football because he has never discovered that the game can be
played with eleven players instead of only five, or in cricket
because he has never moved beyond KwikCrikit played with a
plastic bat and a tennis ball.

The alternative is to realise that we have grown out of childhood spirituality and need something more challenging in our
lives. It takes a child's forthright questions to uncover this truth:
the truth that most of us stay in the nursery when it comes to

thinking about the eternal. Yet it is when we return to the nursery that we are given the chance genuinely to move on into adulthood.

' ... stand back and let them get on with it.'

2

What was the childhood of Jesus like? We have tantalising glimpses from the Gospels. We see Jesus lost on the trip to Jerusalem — and what parent has not shared that heart-stopping moment which hit Mary and Joseph on their way home, when they realised the boy was not

The Alien Game

with them? 'I thought he was with you!' 'No, I thought he was with you!'

At Christmas, preachers sometimes make much of Jesus being born in poverty, but what we know of Joseph and Mary belies this. I have a sneaking suspicion that St Joseph would be extremely annoyed to find his prudent provisions for his son dismissed as 'poverty' by sentimental nineteenth- and twentieth-century clerics keen to point up Jesus' socialist credentials.

Joseph was a skilled craftsman, in one of the few trades that is still in demand two thousand years later; we know that Jesus learned the trade from his father, presumably also inheriting the tools, workshop and business contacts. More significantly, Jesus was sent to learn the holy words of his religion at the feet of the rabbis, not something everyone could afford to do for their son and, in some ways, the first-century equivalent of being sent to a private school.

The evidence suggests that Joseph and Mary were respectable, provident, hard-working people with what would be called good family connections. They were not the richest people on the block, but they were not the poorest either. They set Jesus up with a good start in life. Jesus exhorted his followers to 'leave their families' and give their hearts to God, but in fact one of the most intriguing aspects of the historical Jesus is what he did with the background his parents had provided for him.

He kept in touch with old friends and associates, such as Lazarus, throughout his ministry, yet at the same time he reached out to the poor and dispossessed in radical ways that shocked and surprised those who loved him. He issued the challenge of 'leaving' one's family to follow his path, but he himself did not cut himself off from his family. On the contrary, his own mother remained a steady, watching presence to the end of his life, even suffering the most terrible torture for a parent, that of having to watch her son die in agony.

I used to be very bothered by that radical call to 'turn aside from our families'. It smacked to me of the worst kind of cult leader, enticing young people to follow him to his free-love compound in the middle of the desert, severing connections with families and friends.

Realising what Jesus' words actually meant came, like so many revelations about faith, with parenthood. As I struggled to do the right thing as a parent, I noticed that while the good example of my own parents was a wonderful basis to build on, I could not simply do everything as they had done it. Times had changed and my children were different people. I had to find my own way of bringing up my children. To do so I had to question some of the tenets and structures I had grown up with, ask what they were based on, and eventually chuck one or two of them out because they didn't work for us, or didn't feel right.

To take a very trivial example: to grow up in middle class 1960s Britain was to grow up in a world where class differences were still regarded both as important and as a hugely entertaining spectator sport. Differences in language usage were particularly delighted in. So I grew up hearing popular writers make fun of lower class accents and thought little of it; when I read the journalist Jilly Cooper boasting that her child had said at school,

'My Mummy says "toilet" is a worse word than "f★★★"', I simply thought, 'Yes, of course, and so do I'.

Then my own children grew up in London schools and I very quickly discovered that most London schoolchildren call the WC the 'toilet'. Horror! Was I going to make a stand? Was I going to insist on my children calling it the 'lavatory' or the 'loo'? At first it seemed like an impossible dilemma. Were my children going to grow up with this mark of Cain on their brows? It suddenly hit me — life is too short for this. It does not matter in the slightest what they call it, as long as they know where it is and get there before it is too late. At the same time, I was hearing adults using four-letter words freely in my children's hearing, and the violence and aggression of this kind of language brought home to me that Jilly Cooper was wrong. 'Toilet' is most definitely *not* a worse word than 'f★★★'.

And yet all those years I had been subconsciously dividing the people I met into two groups, 'people who say "toilet"' and 'people who say "lavatory"'. What friendships had this ridiculous division cost me? Whose feelings had I unwittingly hurt? I shall never know, but I was aware that I had wasted mental energy on a silly distinction solely because when I was a child it seemed to be what adults cared about.

I feel that Jesus' radical warning to turn aside from our families and follow him is directed at our hearts. He is asking for a turning-aside that is more akin to the questioning we experience in adolescence than to packing up our backpacks and disappearing to Kathmandu. To become truly his followers we have to stand alone from our families *in our minds*, question our traditions, scrutinise our values and morally re-invent ourselves, every day if necessary.

When our children start questioning our authority in adolescence, there is something of this turning-aside process involved. While it is unbelievably difficult to deal with, adolescent stroppiness has one silver lining to it: it is at least a sign that the youngster is questioning the way things are done. And sometimes their challenges can be useful – as I found with my ridiculous toilet/lavatory dilemma, we can all carry useless mental baggage with us into adulthood.

But the turning-aside process can work for adults too. It can mean standing aside and questioning all that one takes for granted: that might be one's family, but in a wider sense it could mean the broad sweep of the society in which we live. We have to be able to step outside the comforting routine of everyday morality and question it; to question motivations, habits of thought, values, and to ask ourselves, continually, ceaselessly, on what they are based.

The Alien Game

Jesus may have been preaching in particular to a populace accustomed to do certain things because ancestors did them, because they have always been done thus, because the law says things are done thus, because it is written thus. But to follow *his* idea of detachment from our families in the modern world, we have to play a mind-game which you may have played as a child.

This is the game in which you go outside your home and look at it from the other side of the street. You look up at the windows and ask yourself, 'Who lives here?' 'What kind of a family are they?' 'What would I make of them if I knew nothing of them?'

A mother of three told me:

> I used to play this game as a child, with variations. I would stand outside in the garden on a summer night, before the curtains had been closed, and watch the family from outside. Then I would step into the house and pretend to be a stranger, or an alien from another planet, looking at everything as though it were totally unfamiliar.

Play this game and you find yourself asking 'Why?' 'Why are those two children screaming at each other?' 'Why does the mother look so miserable?' 'Why does the father walk in and go straight over to switch on the big box in the corner?'

As an alien, you are not concerned about the material possessions and surroundings of this family. You don't know the difference between a nasty damp patch on the wall and an oil painting, between a costly new hardwood floor and peeling lino. So push to one side any feelings – whether of pride or remorse – prompted by the appearance of your home itself and concentrate on the behaviour of the living creatures inside it.

There is no such thing as a single checklist of 'good parenting' but if you play the alien game, ask yourself some of these questions:

Do I talk with my child, listen to my child, am I patient?

One of those rotten little guilt-inducing facts we read from time to time in the newspapers – along with all the health scares and predictions of catastrophic social disadvantage if your child is bottle-fed/city-dwelling/state-educated/goes to school by car/fails to learn a musical instrument – is that we spend only a few minutes a day on average talking with our children and rarely listen to what they say.

Spending time talking *with* – not at – a child is the simplest, most unarguable building block in creating a happy child. Young children crave practice in talking; older children want to share the ideas bubbling round their heads. A good habit of communication established early in life stays for ever. When the teenage years kick in, it will be a great help to have this long-term habit of talking together firmly established.

There is a simple way to find out if you are spending enough time talking with your child. Aim to spend at least fifteen minutes a day talking together for a week. If fifteen minutes a day is a struggle, then clearly you are not spending enough time on this normally and you need to step it up a bit.

Dr John Henry, an illegal substances expert particularly experienced in spotting illegal drug use, believes that a parent needs to spend 'ten minutes a day' talking with a teenager. He is of the opinion that good communication habits which come from experience are a vital part of the parent's armoury against drug misuse. If you can only manage ten minutes a day for each child, that's still pretty good.

The trouble is – where do we find the time? Well, there is no need to be sitting down in chairs facing each other. Sharing household tasks, driving around in the car, checking through the television magazine together – these are all moments for talking with your child. Snippets of time can add up to ten or fifteen minutes if you look out for the opportunities for listening and talking.

And the key word is – listen! Open your ears and listen to what your child says.

Listening tips

- ✦ **Try to manage without interrupting your child's talk** for as long as possible. With very small children, only interrupt to help supply a word here or to echo a thought there.
- ✦ **Use the psychotherapist's trick of repeating your child's statement back to them**, raising your voice at the end in a question: 'Jessica is a pain, Mum!' 'Jessica is a pain?' 'Yeah, she's got all the others against me in our gang now!' 'She's got all the others against you?' 'Well, Alice and Chloe, mainly. And it's just because I said . . .' And now you will begin to hear the story unfold.
- ✦ **Avoid pushing your opinions, experiences and comments** into your child's conversation for as long as possible. When you do, keep criticism concise and try to balance with a positive remark.
- ✦ **Use direct eye contact** as much as you can (OK, this is difficult when you are driving a car. But not at other times.)
- ✦ And above all: **be patient.**

The world goes much faster than children do. Images flash across the television screen, adults start and finish a conversation before a child has begun to grasp what is going on. It is frustrating for children and can cause them to be angry and to 'close down'. When your children are small, you feel sometimes that your whole life has slowed to an unbearably sluggish pace.

Just a few minutes a day of slowing down to the pace of a small child is a help to both child and parent. But if you are looking after a small child all day it can be very frustrating. The only consolation you can have is that this phase will one day be past and the boot will be on the other foot: you will be rushing to catch up with them.

Am I the one in charge – and am I vigilant?

It's your home: your children are safe here. But they won't be safe unless it is clear who is in charge.

We live in a world where adults are becoming afraid of children. We avoid eye contact with street thugs, even if they are obviously barely out of primary school. We cross the road to avoid gangs of youths and step out of their way. Many men are even afraid to offer to help a distressed child for fear of being accused of child molesting.

Television and Hollywood families routinely show children ruling the roost, snapping back their 'witty' ripostes at parents and mocking any parental attempt at discipline. I am constantly asked by my children, 'Why should I do what you say?' It is a question which would never have occurred to me as a child.

The answer to it is blindingly obvious:

> Because I am your parent, and it is my job to make sure you get the kind of upbringing that will help you be a good person with a fulfilling, worthwhile life. I am your parent and I love you: it is my job to make sure you do as I say.

In their hearts, children know this is true. But they do need to hear you say it once in a while. Because we are inclined to be gentler parents than our grandparents were, because the role models in the media contradict our authority and because children see rebellion rewarded and admired, we are more than ever obliged to be a little bit more vocal about our authority. What used to be taken for granted now needs saying out loud.

Reading the Gospels, I have the impression that Jesus was always surrounded by children, because children were not corralled into the ghetto existence we expect of them now. Jesus lived in a world where children were almost always present: not shoved into schools, crèches and television watching rooms but working and playing alongside their parents.

This is a great difference between 'affluent' Western countries and the Third World today, where life's rhythms are a little closer to the way of life Jesus knew. For us, children are absent from much of life. There are no children in the office, in the factory, in the post room. Children rarely eat in restaurants; they only appear in cafés and 'child-friendly' eateries outside school hours. The first thing I was asked by a well-meaning single friend after the birth of my first child was, 'So how soon can you get away?' Children are regarded as a sideshow to the real business of shopping, earning money and having lunch.

In poorer countries, however, children are on the street for much of the time, either working alongside their parents and relatives or simply running around learning about the world in a haphazard, unstructured way that would make our hair stand on end if we knew the half of it.

When Jesus said, 'Unless you become like children, you will never enter the kingdom of heaven,' he needed a small child to act as a visual aid (probably an audio-visual aid, come to that). I like to think that he only had to stick an arm out and scoop up a passing toddler to make his point. When his disciples got annoyed with the mothers and little ones who were crowding Jesus, he rebuked them gently in what must be among the most famous words he ever uttered, being used as a motto in a thousand Sunday School prints: 'Suffer the little children to come unto me'.

But our children are no longer present in our lives all day; we have to work hard to discover how they are spending their time, to be watchful of what they are doing and the influences affecting them, and to be on the look out for any chance to help a child to learn a lesson from life.

And one aspect of our vigilance is the need to remind children of our authority as parents. Edward Hadas, an American born financial analyst and father of three, gives lectures and talks to parents about using faith as a tool in bringing up children. A problem that strikes him about our modern Western culture is the lack not only of respect for authority but of any idea of what authority is for. After hearing Edward talking very inspiringly to parents about communicating with teenagers, I interviewed him about his faith and its impact on his life. He said:

> Most people are baffled by the whole concept of authority nowadays, they don't understand the notion of an authority that's higher than their own personal good . . . The idea of sacrificing yourself for the sake of your country, for example – totally rejected now. And within the family the notion of some kind of authority which might have traditionally rested in the husband or in the mother – but now that basic concept has been totally rejected and the whole idea of authority has been evacuated.

Reminding our children of our authority does not mean shouting at them, frightening them or punishing them for tiny infringements. It simply means being un-flummoxed by the emotional knife-throwing techniques used by bright, thinking children to get their way.

By 'emotional knife-throwing' I mean those jibes which pin you to the wall and leave you squirming helplessly. Mum remonstrates with her daughter who has left a pile of dirty clothes on the floor: daughter snarls back, 'You don't pick *your* own clothes up every day.'

Mum immediately feels her authority ebb away – it is true, she did leave her clothes on the floor once last week, she was in a hurry to go out. So does this mean she is not qualified to assert her authority over her child? She pauses, backs off and her daughter wins the round. The 'You are no better than I am' knife has skewered her parent.

The daughter's riposte might equally successfully have been: 'You don't ask my brother to pick up his clothes.' It is probably not true but if Mum is not 100 per cent sure, she will be effectively pinned by this knife, the 'unfair' knife.

There are many other knives which can be used to skewer parents emotionally: the 'you don't understand me' knife, the 'no one else's parents are like you' knife . . . the list goes on and on. In our efforts to be fair to our children, and with our horror of overweening authority, we are very easily trapped and pinned to the wall by these knives simply because we are afraid to say,

> Look, what you say is probably true. I am not perfect, I am not always fair though I try to be, and I am not the coolest parent in town. But I am your parent and that gives me the *right* to expect you to obey me; it also *obliges* you to *respect* what I say, even when it is unpalatable.

Do I give my child any responsibility, and what happens if my child gets things wrong?

For very small children, 'helping' is one of the best games of all. In a good nursery, you will always see children helping to tidy up play equipment or clear the dinner table. The trouble with giving children responsibility is that they do not do things always quite as we would, and things do get broken, spilt, lost and generally delayed. It is so much quicker to do it yourself.

One of the most difficult habits to learn as a parent is to

expect children to help or take responsibility for a task and then to stand back and let them get on with it. Your child may mess up the task; what counts is not the mess, but your reaction – is it 'well done for trying' or 'you are hopeless – that's the last time I ask you to do *that!*'

I know I have put some of my own children permanently *off* helping me in the home by being over-critical of their efforts. I know now that when a child folds a sheet badly, the right thing for me to do is quietly to take the sheet and, holding the child's hands, show him once again the right way without a stream of muttered comments. If the child comes to believe that whatever help he tries to give will be inadequate, he will be hiding under his bed every time you seek his assistance.

As parents become less inclined to allow their children the freedom and responsibility of roaming the streets unescorted, giving them responsibility at home becomes incredibly important. For some children, looking after a goldfish or folding up some towels may be the only bit of serious responsibility they get by the age of eight – that's a depressing thought, isn't it?

How's your discipline – all over the place, or consistent, with clear limits?

Single parents say they have a hard time disciplining their children. On the other hand, from the point of view of the two-parent family, it must be nice to have a clear boss – at least the single parent can have everything their own way.

One of the few disadvantages of being a two-parent family is that your discipline can get very muddled: the soft-cop, hard-cop routine is definitely not suitable for bringing up children. Adolf Hitler's background, interestingly enough, fitted the profile of what I consider to be one of the most damaging two-parent family set ups a child can have: a distant, occasionally violent father and a submissive mother who tries to compensate for the father's harshness by being over-indulgent.

The key words to the awe-inspiring task of getting children to do more or less what you want them to do (or at least to avoid doing things you cannot bear the thought of them doing) are 'limits' and 'consistency'. Explain clearly where the boundaries are and what will happen if they are over-stepped: and when the boundaries are over-stepped, do what you threatened to do. To make this work you need to talk together – frequently – about what the limits are, and if necessary thrash out a compromise: and you need to avoid those dreaded Empty Threats, which quickly make a parent into a laughing-stock.

Despite their tough reputation, and despite the fact that certain American Christian 'childcare experts' are positively messianic about the benefits of beating, I have met very few Christian parents who actually use any physical punishment on their children, or think it is a good idea. Very few parents avoid smacking their children completely – I suspect it is a phase even the best parents go through but only on the road to finding less violent sanctions that they can enforce, from simply sending a small child to sit on the stairs for a couple of minutes to withdrawals of privileges, treats, and freedom to go out with friends for older kids and teenagers.

Do you catch your child doing something right?

While you are playing the alien game, watching your family going about its daily business with the eyes of one who had never seen such creatures before, count the number of negative comments you make to your child and compare it with the number of positive comments. Perhaps you find that the numbers are about equal or that the positives outnumber the negatives, but if you find the negatives are in the lead, think hard about the effect this is having on your child.

Would you like to be working for a boss who criticised you more often than he/she complimented you on your work? No, neither would I. Children, even more than adults, need praise in order to build up their confidence and self-esteem. In our rushed and hurried lives it is very easy to remember the one nice remark we said to our child ... and forget the ninety-nine little scolding, hustling, rebuking ones. But the child, on the other hand, remembers the ninety-nine scolding rebukes more keenly than the single kind remark.

When you do have to rebuke your child, separate the behaviour from your child as often as you can. This means being in the habit of saying 'That was a silly thing to do' rather than 'you are a silly girl'. Keep in your head the idea that she's not a silly girl: she is a wonderful girl who has just done something silly.

Don't use sarcasm, or make comparisons with siblings or friends. Above all, don't underestimate how hurtful words can be to a child or a teenager, even to those who are masters of the art of pretending they don't care.

And every now and again, try to catch your child being good, instead of being bad. It's the old, old attention-seeking theory: children like attention and praise, so if you praise the behaviour you want to encourage, they will do more of it. Be vigilant for those moments when your child quietly goes off to make her bed without being asked to, or plays gently with a younger sibling without having a fight.

It is easy to overlook these moments because they attract less attention than the 'bad' behaviour, and in the case of some of my children, any praise for spontaneous bed making is always followed up with 'So can I have next week's pocket money now?' but the basic theory does work. Honest.

Do you stick together as a couple, if you can, and let your child see your love?

'I can't think of anything more warm and secure for a child than to learn how he was conceived,' Pauline, an Anglican mother, once said to me, rather surprisingly. Christian parents are not usually known for their enthusiasm for telling children about sex (another misconception about parents of faith shattered!). 'The idea that you were created by two people loving each other – the two people who love you best of all,' she explained. 'Can there be any more comforting idea for a child?'

A question on a teenage Q and A website, to which teens post their own answers, included the following: 'Name one thing you wish your parents knew about you but you can't bring yourself to tell them.' A boy responded, 'I want them to know that I am still really *bummed* about their divorce, which happened five years ago.'

Being the product of love is indeed a wonderfully comforting idea, and one which young people deeply hate having to give up. And at the moment it still takes a man and a woman to make a child: and as Robert Winston, the IVF guru, has wisely observed, the traditional way of making a baby is always going to be the one people prefer.

Having a mum and a dad who are together remains, unshakeably, the best guarantee in society of a child's happiness, stability and success. Unfortunately, one of the most important tools of bringing children up is one which all too many parents have to do without: namely, the other parent. Many, many lone parents do a great job on their own, working against a terrible list of statistical probabilities.

Children brought up in lone-parent families have less chance of academic success, relationship success and career success than children in stable marriages. Statistics like this do not disclose what we all know – that many lone parents work harder at, and care more about their parenting than some married couples do. But these statistics do show what difficulties such parents have to overcome.

Children need to see how love works. They need to see it in action. They need models to copy. They need to see their parents communicating, co-operating, forgiving, loving, if they are to be able to do these things as adults.

Sexual attraction is instinctive, but falling in love with a kind, loving person is not – the ability to begin and form lasting relationships is something we learn almost entirely from our parents, or other adults close to us. So don't feel shy about hugging or kissing your partner in front of your children – they need to see that hugging does not stop with marriage.

And if praise works with children, it works with partners, too. Do you only ever say critical things about your partner in front of your children? Do you have an exclusively scolding, bantering, sarcastic relationship when they are around, saving your endearments for private moments? Or do you occasionally praise each other: 'This is a lovely dinner', 'Thanks for getting the car serviced', 'You look great today', when your children are in earshot? Play the alien game again: what would the alien see if it could watch you and your partner's behaviour when the kids are around?

Miranda, a single, divorced mother, has taken her young daughters on the same annual Christian family holiday for some years, since her divorce. She is normally the only singleton among many comfortable, happy couples. While other women's strong husbands carry suitcases into the retreat centre, she struggles up the stairs with her own suitcases. She sits alone alongside cosily entwined couples at the prayer and discussion sessions.

When I met her on the same holiday, I eventually plucked up courage to ask her – did she not feel very much the odd one out? Most divorcees, after all, tend to seek the company of other divorcees, don't they? No, not at all. Miranda explained to me why she came.

> Since my husband left our home, my girls don't have a real, living picture of a married couple in front of them any more. So I bring them here every year so that they can see how happily married people behave with each other. I want them to see that marriage *can* work, and to see how people do it. I want them to have some images that they can compare their own relationships with in the future.

My marriage did not work – but I know that marriages can work. I am quite concerned that the girls don't get the idea that because my ex and I didn't get on, it means *no* marriage can work.

Do you enjoy your child?

Yes, I mean just that – enjoying the fact that you have this marvellous gift of a family, that your child is at this magical time of life. If you are a laughing, happy-go-lucky parent who rolls about on the grass with glee, lucky you. You get a lot of fun out of being a parent.

Not all of us find it so easy: we are too busy worrying about money, school, our jobs, our status, our child's last school report, that broken shed window next door that the neighbour *says* was caused by your son's football though you personally are not so sure ... the things that get in the way of enjoying and loving your child are literally endless – and by the time you have got used to worrying about one set of problems, bingo, your child is not a child any more.

Parents who care a lot about their children can easily fall into the trap of regarding their offspring as a chain of problems to be solved. If you can let yourself enjoy your child, you can let yourself have fun at your child's level, play together and be a bit silly together. If you can be your child's playful friend sometimes, you may be more likely to hear some of those secret troubles.

★ ★ ★

This is a book about families who share a faith, but all the questions listed above would be worth asking in any family, believing or not. They are just typical questions that help you to work out any gaps in your parenting.

One thing the alien game can help you do is to see the world not only through the alien's eyes, but through your children's eyes as well. Imagine yourself being a child again, sometimes.

Remember how it felt to be small, to be scared of the dark, to be carsick and yet unable to stop the car from moving, to be confused by something a grown up had said in an angry voice, to be baffled by your maths, to hate lumpy custard. So try being an alien and remember Jesus' terrible curse on anyone who hurt a child — that such a person would be better with a millstone around their neck and thrown into the ocean.

'We are going to pray together every night.'

3

Every night my two youngest children say their prayers. (The older ones are supposed to, as well, but probably do not get round to it as often as I would like.) First the older of the two carefully recites the Lord's Prayer, very correctly, and gives me a big hug. Then the youngest puts her hands

All About Prayer

together and recites her favourite prayer, in a special staccato 'praying voice', where all the words begin with capital letters, like this:

> Father In Heaven, I Come To Say,
> Thank You For Your Love Today.
> Thank You For My Family,
> And All The Friends You Give To Me.
> Guard Me In The Dark Of Night,
> And In The Morning Send Your Light,
> *Amen*.

Or else she makes up a prayer of her own, a bravura performance built of key 'prayer-type' words, words which she has noticed grown-ups using in these situations: a typical *extempore* composition might go like this:

> Oh Jesus, help me to be good, give all the people in the whole world your Spirit, and God is very special, and Jesus is very special, and the Spirit is very special, and look after everybody in the whole world with the Spirit.

Then she adds her own robust, double-fisted version of the sign of the cross, which goes, 'In-a-name-of-the-father-son-an-hoe-spit-

amen'. Then, with sudden decisiveness, she dives under the bed-
clothes giggling with pleasure at a job well done.

I know a lot of Christians would shake their heads at this
ritual and say, 'She is not really praying; she is parroting words she
has heard adults use.' Other Christians would say, 'You are not
teaching her enough reverence. You should not let her say the
words incorrectly.'

Prayer is like dieting or giving up smoking. Firstly, it is a learning experience: no one can be sure of getting it right first time.
And one day of it is not enough. To make a difference, you have
to stick at it for a long, long time.

Teresa Crabtree, a mother of eleven who is also an inspira-
tional Sunday School teacher, remembers:

> When I started praying with my two eldest they wouldn't
> even sit still and I made them sit on a special cushion – it
> took a year before they would behave – we lit candles and
> they blew them out.

But unlike dieting or fitness regimes, prayer does not thrive on
becoming automatic, something you do 'without thinking'.
Though there are believers who are convinced that the very act
of reciting set prayers is powerful in itself, most Christians think
of prayer as a personal dialogue with God. And once you have
begun to exchange dialogue 'without thinking' it is still friendly
but eventually slips towards the meaninglessness of an on-hold
phone message that promises, 'Our operators are waiting to serve
you' when they are quite clearly not.

The hardest idea to get across to children about prayer is that
while it can be a powerful tool in building up the child's own
understanding of spirituality, in creating a conversation with
God, to be powerful, it has to be both routine *and* spontaneous.
The familiar formulas that Christian parents have taught their
children for generations are a framework, but they need pepping
up with personal prayer as well, in thought if not in word.

There are two big mistakes we make in teaching children how

to pray. Some parents concentrate too much on teaching old-fashioned prayer formulas – sets of comforting nursery words that help us to avoid facing the duty of using the language of worship for ourselves. This habit keeps prayer in the nursery and never lets it out. At the other extreme, many new-style Christian parents over-emphasise the spontaneity of prayer and leave the child floundering, making everything up as he or she goes along. The strong, ancient formulas – the 'magic words' – that resonate with centuries of Christianity are forgotten.

Surprisingly late in the day, medical researchers have got round to examining the power of regular, routine prayer. A study reported in the *British Medical Journal* (22/29 December 2001) looked closely at the effect of reciting either the Rosary or yoga mantras on the praying person's 'cardiovascular rhythms'.

The Rosary is the Roman Catholic repetitive cycle of meditation consisting of three sets of five 'decades' of prayers, top-and-tailed by the Creed and other special prayers. Each set of decades is devoted to a 'mystery' – a key event in the lives of Christ and the Virgin Mary.

The formula has variations but in general each decade is made up of the Lord's Prayer, a 'Glory Be', a short prayer beginning 'O My Jesus' and ten – yes, ten – repetitions of the 'Hail Mary'. In one set of five Mysteries, therefore, the praying person says the Hail Mary fifty times, which, with the other prayers in the cycle, can take between fifteen minutes to half an hour, depending on the speaking speed.

The researchers, from the University of Pavia, Italy, found that the breathing rhythm of the 'Hail Mary' corresponded exactly with the six-breaths-per-minute rhythm recommended for inducing physiological effects that increase 'calmness and well-being'. The researchers did not reveal whether they thought the recital of the Rosary in Italian – as opposed to any other language – was crucial to the effect, but they added:

We believe that the Rosary may have partly evolved because it synchronised with the inherent cardiovascular (Mayer) rhythms, and thus gave a feeling of wellbeing, and perhaps an increased responsiveness to the religious message.

In other words, praying can be seriously good for your health.

But like dieting and fitness programmes (at least in my experience), indeed like anything supposed to be good for your health, prayer habits that are doomed to fail if they start out with good intentions that stretch the possible beyond the practical. 'OK, kids,' you say brashly one day, 'from now on we are *The Waltons*. We are *Little House on the Prairie*. We are going to pray together every night.' And you manage it for a couple of nights. It is very sweet to watch. The children fold their hands and say, 'God bless Mummy and Daddy, God bless Granny,' in singsong voices.

Then on the third night, maybe, you go out for the evening and are too shy to ask the babysitter to say prayers with the children. On the fourth night, one child goes on a sleepover and by the time you remember about the prayer thing, the other child has fallen asleep. The night after that, you are feeling just too busy, or just too grumpy, and it all seems a bit pointless.

Besides, praying with your children is such a self-conscious affair: moving from a normally completely informal household atmosphere into the formal, even artificial atmosphere of a prayer session is not easy to do. So you forget all about it. Six months later you have another try, feeling even more self-conscious and false. The same thing happens.

The only way to cope with a string of false starts like this is to ask yourself what the praying is supposed to be *for*. We hear people talking about praying nearly every day: 'We just have to hope and pray . . .' is a common expression. It is gradually coming to mean no more than 'I don't really think this longed-for outcome is going to happen'.

Ask yourself and your child – do we pray to . . .

✦ Get God to do something for us?
✦ Create a warm fuzzy atmosphere at bedtime?
✦ Or is it to build a dialogue with the spiritual entity we call the Divine?

Most children will say that they pray to God to ask him to do something for them. 'Whatever you ask in prayer, believe that you receive it, and you will' (Mark 11:24). Children accept this as obvious but to adult ears it sounds intolerably glib. Perhaps it is easier for us to deal with the idea that God listens to, and answers prayers in different ways.

Charlotte, mother of three daughters, is aware of the pitfalls of praying with your children:

> When my father was very ill my elder daughter remarked that she would think badly of God if he let Grandpa die. I realised she was still at the stage of thinking you can make bargains with God. I am very wary of that idea. So when I pray with the children it's usually more about saying thank you. It's about celebration and gratitude and awareness of what we have been given, rather than asking for specific things.

Discuss the idea of prayers, which are sincerely felt, which come from your *heart* – as opposed to 'shopping list' prayers. Yes, God does answer all prayers – but they have to be 'proper' prayers, not extensions of your Christmas wish list. The prayer 'Please God let me have a new games console,' may express a desire of unbearable intensity at the moment the child utters it; but the chances are that last year the same intensity went into a prayer for the less glamorous version of the toy which is now gathering dust, ignored, on the play-cupboard shelf.

And whereas God does answer all prayers, he has a number of ways of doing so. You don't always get what you ask for, but *the very act of prayer helps us to understand our predicament, to take stock of our abilities and powers.* And most of the time this understanding is in itself an answer to prayer.

I reckon I have counted four ways, so far, in which God answers prayers. There may be others, but I think I have identified the following as the most common 'answers' to prayer:

'Yes'

It does happen. Of course, according to the laws of probability, prayer would have to be 'answered' some of the time even if there were no God, because quite often what people want to happen, happens. But people who have felt touched by prayer will tell you that it happens not according to the law of probability, at least not obviously so. I have many friends who, shyly and with wonderment, have recounted extraordinary personal tales of prayers answered – stories that, if they are only delightful coincidences, are nonetheless delightful. Answered prayer happens sometimes in the most ridiculously trend-bucking way, as though God were playing games with us.

Perhaps we are just people that nice things happen to ... or perhaps prayer helps us to make the good things happen for ourselves, or for those we care about. Either way, it works.

'Later'

Some Christians believe that God answers all sincere prayers – *in the end.* This is the kind of unanswerable, unshiftable, infuriating, jam-tomorrow-but-never-jam-today faith that makes atheists want to tear their hair out.

'No'

Personally I think he uses this one quite a lot. God's obvious answer to: 'Can you make sure that my best friend gets spots this weekend, as I want to get off with her boyfriend?' or 'Can I have a new pair of Reeboks?' is 'No.'

And last but not least:

'No, You Do It'

I get this answer rather often, too. This is the feeling that steals up on you in moments of deep prayer, when you are tussling with an intractable problem or difficult dilemma. Deep in your heart you know that you must make the first move to resolve the problem or extricate yourself from the horns of the dilemma. And in the middle of your heartfelt appeals to God to sort it all out for you, you hear a tough, little voice saying, 'No, you do it.' *No, you* make the first move to mend that rift with your friend. *No, you* sit down with your teenage son to talk about his dubious new circle of friends. *No, you* re-train to get a better paid job. *No, you do it* is the answer you get when you are trying to walk away from a duty, but disguising it as handing things over to God.

★ ★ ★

Try talking with your children about the different ways God might answer prayers. Above all emphasise that your child should aim at a conversation with God. Try to get away from their childish idea of God as an old man in heaven guarding an inexhaustible supply of crisps, trips to Euro Disney and new clothes, which he will hand out to children who say their prayers.

How to Pray with Your Children

Here is what Ram Gidoomal, leader of the Christian People's Alliance, a multi-denominational political party based in London, says about prayer with his three (now grown-up) children:

At home prayer time has always been crucial. For one thing, we always pray at mealtimes – and even if the children have been having a battle just before the meal. We pray in restaurants, never mind the embarrassment of having all eyes upon us: and as well as thanking God for the food we usually bring in other issues as well as part of our prayer.

At bedtime we have a ritual that the children insisted on for many, many years: it is called Sad, Bad and Glad.

It works like this. The child tells you – and God – about something sad that happened that day; then something which they did which was bad, however tiny; and lastly something which happened which made them feel glad. We offer these experiences up to God, ask forgiveness for the bad thing and thank Him for the 'glad' thing. It is a simple prayer formula and it has served us very well over the years. A few years after we started this ritual we reached the point where none of the children would agree to go to sleep without it!

Ram was deeply moved, years later, to discover that his son, now in his twenties, was using 'Sad, Bad and Glad' as an ice-breaker in church youth sessions.

Lizzie, a mum of two under-fives, has worked out her bedtime prayer routine with her four-year-old.

She thinks of one thing she most wants to thank God for that happened that day, usually something to do with a person rather than sweets or treats. Then we do God Bless – anyone in hospital, people who are dead and in heaven. Then we say a prayer she learned at school: she loves making the sign of the cross, which she has recently learned.

Teresa Crabtree, whose eleven children make an awe-inspiring little prayer group, likes to make prayer time as physically different and ritualistic as possible:

Have as many candles as you like – they are very in fashion, they make a big difference. Have a crucifix or a picture of Jesus that you can all look at. The important thing about prayer is regularity. Aim for five minutes at least once a day. It's actually very difficult and everything else gets in the way, preparing lunch boxes, for example. I ask the children to remind me that we have to pray: I want them to see that I would rather we were a bit rushed for school than that we went to school without our morning prayers.

Morning prayers? Why not? Bedtime is not the only time you can pray with children. One mother wrote:

When my children were facing school and its potential challenges, an elderly woman in our church suggested that we pray every morning before they left for school. Amazingly, this relaxed me as a parent and it gave my children freedom from fear.

The Gidoomals pray in the morning too – this is when Ram and his wife Sunitra pray most intensively together. No time to pray in the mornings? Do it on the run, like Greg and Agghi Clovis. Getting ten children out of the house to school and college every morning is, as you can imagine, something resembling a small military operation for this extraordinary South London family. Agghi says:

We pray on the way to school. We drive past a church each day and as we drive along, we offer up whatever are the issues of the day: one child has a test coming up, another is trying to patch up a quarrel with a friend, whatever is on our minds.

Teresa Crabtree, on the other hand, finds praying in the car 'too distracting' so it probably depends on how good a driver you are – and on whether you have a fast whiz through country lanes or a slow crawl through outer London traffic jams.

Praying and reading the Bible

Another family of Charismatic Catholics I know not only have share powerful prayer times together but also sometimes think together about a Bible passage that seems special for the day. The lynchpin of the tradition is Olive, now a grandmother, who has insisted for years that her active, down-to-earth family have a moment of intense spirituality once in the day.

Many of the Christian families I have met have impressed me with their enthusiasm for reading the Bible with their children. This enthusiasm is not necessarily confined to the believing members of the family. As Charlotte says:

> Oddly enough, the person who has taught my three daughters more about the Bible than anyone is my husband, Mark, who is a total agnostic bordering on atheist. He is a journalist and he loves reading the Bible to them: it is something he began doing regularly when they were quite small. I think he just adores the language and the narrative force of the stories.

I admit I do not find it easy to pick up a Bible and read out part of the Gospel to my children at bedtime. Instead I choose one of a range of bright and cheerful picture books with simply told versions of the stories. A cop-out? Definitely. But better than nothing.

As children grow older, it becomes more difficult to involve them in reading the Bible, as a rule. However I know families who manage to carry it through – the older kids enjoy choosing passages for themselves and reading them out to the rest of the family.

Praying for special things

'Our youngest had a serious bowel complaint as a baby – he needed a series of operations,' said Diana, mother of two young adults and two adopted children. 'When he started crying we would gather round and put our hands on him and pray for the pain to be taken away. And it always worked.'

I am a bit sceptical about prayer as a cure for physical illness. But I meet so many Christian families whose lives have been turned around by the healing power of prayer that I can only stand humbly in amazement. Certainly such experiences draw families closer together.

Andrea's eight-year-old son and ten-year-old daughter were both plagued with a congenital digestive malfunction that limited their diet drastically. As a last resort, Andrea took the children to a healing session at a local church; the church community prayed for the children's health and within a few weeks the problem, which had plagued the family since these two youngsters were babies, disappeared and never returned.

Whether or not this was a result of prayer is really irrelevant; more interesting is that Andrea and her family have over the years developed a powerful personal relationship with God partly as a result of it – and their personal relationship with God is a marvellous guiding factor for them.

Both these families pray together habitually – it is something they have learned to do because they find it works. Diana's family are Charismatics and, she admitted to me rather shyly, pray in tongues, which is a terribly un-English thing to do. Andrea's older children have long conversations late into the evening about God and even pray together. They are also perfectly normal, occasionally stroppy, forgetful, late-sleeping, computer-hogging teenagers.

Bad prayer habits

I know that many people would say that my youngest child's idea of 'praying' is not worth the time it takes because she does not 'understand what the words mean'. Here is the literary critic Lorna Sage, expressing the typical modern liberal distaste for the practice of learning prayers by rote in her account of being a pupil at a 1950s village primary school:

> First there was dinner money, then the register. Then Miss Myra would hang up a cracked oilcloth scroll with the Lord's Prayer printed on it in large curly letters. She prompted, we mumbled our way through, getting out of sync during the trespasses and catching up with each other to arrive in unison at 'For ever and ever. Amen.' . . . Soon you'd be able to recite 'Our Father' and the multiplication tables with sing-song confidence, hitting the ritual emphasis right: 'And *twelve* twelves are a *hundred* and forty-*four. Amen.*'
>
> (*Bad Blood,* Fourth Estate, 2000)

We all have heard funny stories of children mangling well-known prayers such as the Lord's Prayer: 'Lead us Not Into Thames Station' (*lead us not into temptation),* 'Forgive us Our Press Passes' *(forgive us our trespasses)* and so on.

But in schools or other places where children say prayers regularly, the repeated formulas have a binding force beyond 'what the words mean'. The prayer at the beginning of the day or just before lunch serves to punctuate the school day, to put a marker down showing that it is time to move on to the next stage. Hearing the words again in later life can bring the senses and sounds of a whole era flooding into the brain. This kind of ritual is deeply comforting to children, and sensitive writers such as Lorna Sage are aware of its value, but in passages such as the one I have just quoted she also allows us to see her contempt for by-rote prayer learning: she thinks that chanting words that mean nothing to the chanter is not an uplifting experience. But I would contend that such chanting has its place in a child's spiritual growth.

Just as religion is close – for some people, worryingly close – in children's minds to magic, so prayers are easily confused with magic spells. Children know at once that words are powerful –

don't they spend most of their time learning to use them? They therefore have a strong tendency to imbue words with magical significance.

A road safety researcher once told me that when small children first learn how to cross the road, they may quickly pick up the dangerous idea that formulas such as 'Look right, look left, look right again . . . ' are not mnemonics but *spells* which will ward off cars if repeated on the kerb. A small child may not put it quite this way, but will certainly mutter the words while standing on the kerb, swivelling his head ritually from right to left without actually *seeing* if the road is clear or not.

The same kind of misunderstanding can easily arise with prayers. Teaching children prayers by means of simple, regular repetition is not a difficult thing to do (and small children absorb words like a sponge). Early familiarity with the words frees the child later to move more easily onto the next step, the task of meditating on the meaning of the words. But the child seems almost inevitably to have to pass *through* a phase of regarding the prayer as a magic spell, to be muttered as fast as possible under the blankets to ward away monsters at night.

I never discourage my youngest from her decidedly hammy displays of piety. She feels good about doing it, she enjoys it, and it allows her to keep me by her bedside for another few minutes. Of course she is 'parroting'. I do not pretend to myself that her praying is much more than a dialogue with herself, at this moment. I know perfectly well that Agatha is not 'lifting her mind and heart to God' in precisely the way intended by the definition of prayer in the Catholic catechism. I know perfectly well that she has only the tiniest inkling of what the sign of the cross means. I *know* her praying is not ideal.

But I also believe that she needs to pass through the 'magic spell' phase of praying in order to reach the deeper understanding that lies on the other side. She is enjoying the sensations of prayer and revelling in the idea of having a dialogue with some amazing divine person called God. If I can get her to think about this, even tangentially, for a couple of minutes a day I know I am laying the foundations of faith.

Added to which, the idea of prayer as a regular act is being embedded in my daughter's daily life at an early age. One day, she will have to re-invent her entire concept of prayer. One day, she will challenge the prayers she learned from me, perhaps put them aside, perhaps even put aside the concept of prayer altogether. But the habit, should she wish to return to it, will be there, waiting, and the formulas will be there for her to work with and on.

Already she has chosen her own pattern of praying – to use a fixed prayer followed by a spontaneous prayer. Already she feels happy and comfortable with her praying. My role is to try, over the years ahead, to move her on to the next stage, which is why I often say, if I feel she is thinking a little harder about the prayer than usual; 'I think God was listening very carefully to your prayer.' This is why we sometimes go over the day's events and think of things that have happened we would like to offer up to God because they are troubling or happy.

Making fun of the family prayer time is a different matter. It is hard to know how strict to be when, for example, my child does her own upside-down, two-handed take on the Sign of the Cross. Olive says:

> If they start mucking about and making fun of prayer time, then I say – OK, you are on your own, kid. In the end they usually come back to it. We try to make prayer time a really quality time together, a happy shared moment.

The plus side of much-derided 'parroting' of set-piece prayers like the Rosary is a way of demanding a space for prayer. Mentally, the praying person is arranging the furniture of her brain so that prayer has somewhere to 'sit down'. And if you are saying set-piece prayers with children, you always have the option to be creative with prayer, turning the prayer time into a constant dialogue with God by bringing in the child's own ideas and experiences. 'Often, half way through prayers,' says one mother who organises regular set prayers with her children, 'they want to talk about something that happened that day – and five minutes of prayer becomes twenty-five minutes of discussion.'

Ram Gidoomal's 'Sad, Bad, Glad' routine is followed by many parents, with variations. One version is 'two things about my day': ask the child to think of two significant things that happened that day, one pleasant, one not so pleasant. There will always be something to put into each category. Together, ask for help, or forgiveness, for the not-so pleasant event and give thanks for the happier memory.

How to make up a prayer

If your child has learned about writing letters, he or she probably knows that there are formal ways of laying out a letter – standard patterns that everyone recognises. Your child will also recognise that the way a letter is laid out is less important than what the letter says. The layout just helps to get the message over.

A prayer can be made up in any way you like – what matters is that it is a sincere dialogue with God. But it is helpful to have a framework for 'laying out' your prayers.

One simple formula is the four-point ACTS checklist:

◆ Adoration
◆ Confession
◆ Thanks
◆ Supplication

Adoration is the part that causes most distrust among non-Christians. 'I don't like the way God seems to need to be adored and praised,' said Tony Robinson, the English comic actor. This is a very British response. We don't like show-offs and we don't like sycophants.

But if you cannot bring yourself to contemplate the awesome

idea of a creative Deity, then you are in danger of putting yourself at the centre of your universe – and that way lies complete selfishness. For small children, it takes a massive effort of imagination *not* to put oneself at the centre of the universe. For them, 'adoration' in the context of prayer need only mean thinking something like – 'I am very small, and God is very big and powerful – and He loves me!'

Adoration is when your praying lifts you out of yourself; when you remind yourself that there is more out there. It is not sycophancy or fawning. And God only needs it because He needs you to accept the truth.

The second part of any good, rounded prayer is *confession*. Every Church has some form of confession – the vital act of 'owning up' to what we have done wrong. Just doing this, and doing it sincerely, is one of the most obviously therapeutic aspects of religion.

Most people, and many Christians, shy away from the Catholic idea of a personal sacrament made directly to a priest; there are endless myths about this practice, most perpetuated by television and Hollywood, and non-Catholics widely believe that the practice gives the priest some kind of sinister 'power' over people. This may have been true once upon a time: rich families of Renaissance Venice were always careful to go to a confessor who was also a relative, so as to keep their sins 'in the family', which does suggest that they feared that confessing to an unknown priest would make hostages of their sins.

Yet even critics of the practice of 'going to confession' would admit that owning up for what you have done wrong is a good idea; and we live in a remarkably confessional age, though tabloid newspapers and the people who feed them 'confessions' sometimes make little distinction between confession and bragging.

If your prayer is to be a genuine conversation with God, it needs to be on an honest footing, with nothing hidden. That makes sense to everyone.

Thanks make up the third part of prayer. Look around at what you have, before moaning about what you don't have. Give thanks for health, for family and friends, for the world, the spring, your football team – the longer the list, the more the act of thinking of the wonderful things that the world has to show will lift your spirits towards God.

Lastly comes the part where you moan about what you do not have: *supplication* – 'asking for stuff'. Most people begin praying when they have problems, not when everything is going well, and most people think of praying as issuing God with a shopping list. Far too many prayers are shopping lists left on God's kitchen counter, reading, 'Go out and get me this, this and this. And while you are about it, the kitchen floor could do with a wipe.'

Children inevitably start praying on these terms. But praying when we feel the need for something is not enough. It is a good sign if you and your child start praying at other times, too.

Evangelical families are sometimes encouraged to keep 'prayer journals', or 'prayer notebooks' in which the family can record each family member's prayer requests. Such journals might note down which days a particular item has been prayed for, when the prayer was answered and so on.

A prayer journal is a charmingly literal interpretation of the idea of prayer, and one that is a real test of faith. I have not experimented with it myself – I can just imagine my elder daughter going through the book in disgust, pointing to each apparently 'unanswered' prayer in turn – 'That didn't happen. That didn't. That turned out to be a disaster.' She would then close the book, and peer at God severely over the top of her glasses: 'All in all, this is a very poor record, God.'

However this is a sign of my poor faith. Teresa Crabtree's children take great delight in pointing out examples to each other of answered prayers: 'Look, I found my pen, because we prayed for me to find it, didn't we?' Teresa feels they will never forget those moments.

One day I might summon up the courage to keep a prayer

journal. If you do, much thought has to be given to following up each prayer intention with further prayer and consideration, and you need to be prepared to keep the prayer journal active for many, many years. The notebook should contain ample space to write down any comments or afterthoughts about the prayer itself, whether or not the writer felt it was worthwhile or sincere, and to ask tough questions about the aftermath.

So if a child prays for her birthday party to be a success, one day she can return to that page in the prayer notebook and write down what happened. If the party was not a success, because the birthday girl threw a tantrum and had to be sent off to bed early, ask the child, 'was the failure of this prayer request really God's fault?' Did God in fact give you the tools to make events unfold as you wanted, only to see you misuse the tools, or fail to realise they were there?

The prayer journal might be interesting, but it should never be used as evidence for or against God's efficiency. Only a very primitive idea of God presents the deity as an arm of the service industry. Prayer journals no doubt work for those who use them, but personally I fear that the idea comes close to 'putting God to the test'.

Prayable moments

As well as building a workable routine of prayer into your life, look for 'prayable' moments. Is it sunny? Say, 'Thank you God for this wonderful weather.' Did you catch the train by a whisker? Say, 'Let's thank God that our legs were fast enough to carry us down that station platform!'

Disappointments should be prayable moments – when your child's school team goes belly up on the football field, in the car on the way home say, 'Let's ask God to help us cope with losing the match'.

Praying in the morning is so good. You feel stronger, focussed, and more capable of meeting the day's challenges. We remind ourselves of the good intentions we fell asleep with.

Do you pass a church on any regular walk – to school or to the park? 'We often pop into the church on our way home from school to light a candle for anyone we want to think of specially,' says Lizzie.

If you have older children who squabble, try asking them to pray with you next time they are rowing with each other. Do not expect an instant response – persist.

Pray when you are about to set out for a family holiday, or when any family member is about to go off on some adventure such as a guide camp, college interview or inter-school sports fixture. Just briefly link hands and say a few words. When we have done this we find the squabbles dry up for quite a while. Prayer works as a source of inner examination as well as a gateway for illumination from the outside.

Above all, pray not only when things are going wrong but when things are going right. 'When bad things happen, such as bereavement, people always start looking around for God,' Diana mused. 'They instinctively feel. "I can't deal with this on my own".' The trouble for most people is that they do not have the habit of prayer, the habit of opening up their consciences and minds, so on the whole they do not get a response. But if your children have a framework for praying and do not feel awkward about it, they will have a precious spiritual advantage over the rest of the world. Which sounds worth working for, doesn't it?

'The fatso in the red suit takes up a lot of space ...!'

4

It's Christmas. For once in your life as a Christian parent, the world, while not exactly dancing to your tune, at least is humming it. Not to mention playing it over the radio, in the shopping centre, the lift and every public place where a syncopated sub-jazz rendering of 'Hark the Herald Angels Sing' can be piped.

We Wish You a Merry Advent

Well, actually, if we are talking about most of December, it is not Christmas. It is Advent. The distinction between preparing for Christmas and the festival itself, weird mishmash of sacred, profane and conspicuous consumption that it is, has been scuffed and blurred over the years.

Christmas — or Advent — is one time of year when even the most cynical child can, albeit grudgingly, see the point of being Christian. It is the one season when a Christian child feels that the whole world is acknowledging the validity of the family's faith instead of walking roughshod over it. From time to time on television your child may hear brief but distinctly audible references to Jesus, the Nativity, even Bethlehem. Faith gets a cool, but not always entirely discourteous, nod from the media.

The Christian child can, with a little parental support, even go so far as to feel that at Christmas time, it is much more fun to belong to a faith than to belong to none. There are more

rituals, more delightful little surprises to look forward to, a shape
and purpose to the whole thing. While your child's friends for
most of the time denounce churchgoing as boring and religion
as irrelevant, the excitement of a midnight Mass service or the
charm of a nativity scene have a glamour of their own.

It is worth taking a bit of trouble over Christmas memories,
because the memories you make for your child at Christmas will
one day play a part in her or his spiritual life. The childish long-
ing for new toys and delicious things to eat becomes gloriously
mixed up with the Advent and Incarnation of Our Lord to produce a shiver of delight in later years. This happy muddling-up of
the childish and the sacred is to be treasured, not censured. Other
religions have traditions which fire children's imaginations: the
Jewish tradition of Rosh Hashanah, for example, when families
recall the wanderings of the Israelites in the wilderness by spending the night either in the open air (or, more usually in northern
climates, out in a covered porch or conservatory, bundled up
among pillows and duvets) is full of excitement and wonder.

So let's look at how you can keep your Christmas Christian –
so that in bleaker times when your child is an adult, perhaps
wandering away from faith, once a year happy memories of the
awe and excitement of a truly Christian Christmas will keep
whispering to her or him: 'Come back, come back.'

You can't do everything at once. But you can focus on these
four ideas:

✦ **Follow the Christian timetable,** not the High Street's. Put
the Church's preparations and celebrations at the top of your
priority list.
✦ **Build up traditions** within your family which mesh in with
those of the Church.
✦ **Manage the gift-giving process** to encourage thoughtful-
ness and discourage greed. Put Santa in his place.
✦ **Encourage children** to think of the nativity as a real event,
not a fairy story.

Building your Christmas round the Church

Your child will not get the message about the Christian nature of Christmas if churchgoing is an optional add-on. If you have not yet got to grips with being a regular church-goer, then Advent – the four Sundays before Christmas – is a perfect time to start visiting some local churches. If you like the way they 'do' Christmas, you have an idea of whether they will suit you otherwise.

Do not expect a wonderful spiritual experience if you just turn up out of the blue at a strange church on Christmas Eve or Christmas Day. You are bound to feel out of things. The distinguished and intelligent British actress Imogen Stubbs tried such last-minute 'church tasting' one Christmas, her undefined longings for a spiritual life prompted by her children's artless questions. But, as the article she wrote about the experience for the *Daily Telegraph* revealed, she was constantly distracted by the externalities of the services she visited: the video screens at a noisy Evangelical meeting, the unfamiliar bread in a Russian Orthodox church, a mobile phone ringing in a Catholic church. The novelty, for Stubbs, of being inside a church after twenty years' absence was so great that she seemed to find it very difficult to open herself up to whatever it was she was looking for. She concluded, thoughtfully but a little sadly:

> In truth, I found myself responding to location and theatricality rather than content because I still find religious certainty enviable but unsettling. But I also now recognise that at different stages in our brief lives we need solace and guidance to help us brave the secret and undiscovered road ahead of us . . . we should introduce our children to every kind of religion and let them decide.

In other words, 'never mind about *my* faith, *my* spiritual longings – it's all for the children really'. But if she remains hovering around the edges of different 'brands' of Christianity, not willing to commit to any of them, are her children being told that faith matters – or not?

Stubbs felt, as many of us do at Christmas, that there must be 'something in it'. If you are not churchgoers but would like to 'try' a church, don't just turn up on spec: do a recce on the phone. When planning Christmas treats and socialising, make sure at least one activity is God-centred – a carol concert, Handel's *Messiah*, a church carol service. Think also about a charitable activity that the children can take part in – if you live in a city where there are homeless or roofless people, for example, older children and teenagers can be quite useful taking a turn on a volunteer rota at a hostel or free-meal service. Younger children can join in carol singing for a charity. There is always something you can do if you look for it.

Start late and separate Advent from Christmas

Has Christmas really become more tawdry than it used to be? I suspect it always was pretty tacky – it's just that now it is tacky for longer.

I like to think of modern Christmas as dating from 1867, the first year the New York department store Macy's stayed open until midnight on Christmas Eve, forever altering the meaning of the term 'Christmas vigil' and switching the balance between commerce and religious observance. Since then the only direction in which shops could extend the Christmas shopping period has been backwards, and so they have, with Christmas trees appearing in shop windows before the hideous Hallowe'en masks have been taken down.

Where I live, it is normal for shops to have their Christmas decorations up from mid-October. The practice never seems to improve business significantly: how much we spend at Christmas seems to have more to do with the state of interest rates on our credit cards than anything the retail sector does. Early Christmas preparations succeed thoroughly, on the other hand, in killing off any residual delight and wonder that might still linger in our jaded urban hearts. It is very hard to feel excited about an ambiguously labelled 'holiday season' which lasts for more than one-sixth of the year.

So the Christmas decorations are usually looking rather sad when Christmas Day actually dawns. To wait until Twelfth Night (6 January), to take them down is for many people unbearable and they cannot wait to get rid of them. Then there are the school activities. Suppose your child's school term ends on around 15 December. Christmas concerts, nativity plays and other stuff have to be performed in the middle of Advent (and of course rehearsed from September); Christmas dinners may be served a fortnight before the end of term. The earlier your child's Christmas holidays begin, the earlier Christmas starts.

It is as though the whole world has lost the ability to look forward to anything, to defer gratification. By the time Christmas Day arrives, there is nothing left to do. We have sung *Away in a Manger* dozens of times. The school nativity play was so long ago that we have almost forgotten it. We have been trying to eat up the same Christmas cake for weeks. In fact, by New Year's Eve, we are completely sick of Christmas, and it is barely ten months before the whole thing starts all over again.

When one day, as I predict it will, it becomes standard practice to open Christmas presents at any time during December, so that disappointing items or wrongly-sized garments can be taken back to the shop and exchanged, then the secularisation of Christmas will have achieved the ultimate aim of abolishing the last little scrap of self-discipline left to give this winter festival any kind of special character at all.

Sticking to the Church's own calendar will make your child's (and even your own) experience of Christmas more meaningful and more exciting. Don't just move through Advent – what television people now call 'the run-up to Christmas' (the playwright Alan Bennett once noted in his diary that Lent had become 'the run-up to Easter') as though it were an extension of Christmas

Day. Instead, live Advent, prayerfully. Advent has a special character of its own – separate it in your mind from Christmas and give it its due.

Don't rush in with the tinsel

When I was a child my Christmas Eve job was to decorate our tiny tree, using the same glass baubles year after year. We listened to the Nine Lessons and Carols from King's College, Cambridge on the radio at the same time.

Because they were old, the tree decorations were full of family history. They included some amazingly grotty cardboard ones which, my mother explained, were 'Austerity' Christmas decorations: all that were available during World War II. They also included a tiny glass giraffe with a broken leg, for which no one has ever been able to give an adequate explanation. There was something fascinating about re-using these ridiculous little scraps of our past, pulling them out of their box at the same time on the same day every year.

A church where the Christmas season is observed properly seems peculiarly drab and ordinary to a child's eye during Advent. Yet how much more magical still is that moment on Christmas Eve, or early on Christmas morning, when the child enters the church to find it transformed and glittering with candle-light: how much more dramatic the Nativity scene is if it is kept veiled until just the right moment. And how magical is a Christmas tree which suddenly lights the darkness of the living room at tea-time on Christmas Eve.

If your children find it hard to wait until Christmas Eve, why not compromise by waiting at least until the first day of the Christmas school holidays? Fix on a date as your Tree Day and stick to it in years to come – bingo, you have made a tradition. If there is a birthday or other family anniversary in the week before Christmas, use this as your special decorations day.

Making the Most of Advent

The great clear-out day

It has been estimated that the average family with children under sixteen has in the region of £280 worth of toys in the house that no one plays with, no one wants and no one would miss. I am not sure what the researchers who winkled that fact out meant by 'worth'. Jesus told us to sell all we had and follow him: but we must accept that things held their value better in those days – the market for second-hand carpenter's tools in 30 AD was probably a lot healthier than the twenty-first century market for Lego pirate ships with a quarter of their pieces missing.

Rather than selling all they have, then, invite your children to pile it all into three mountains called 'Keep', 'Good Enough To Give' and 'Total Junk'. The last-named includes toys that are broken or irredeemably incomplete and ends in the bin. The first pile will include some things the children had forgotten they owned, and which will enjoy a renaissance now that the junk under which they were hidden has gone.

The key pile is, of course, the 'Good Enough to Give' pile. Somewhere in your area there must be an institution which can use second-hand toys in good, safe condition – a family centre, a children's home, a hospital.

Our children's school runs a second-hand toy stall each Christmas: it is a great way of offloading the outgrown stuff in a good cause, and since everything is sold wonderfully cheaply, my children can take the opportunity to buy each other Christmas presents with their own pocket money. This terrific arrangement only occasionally backfires when they walk away from the stall minus their pocket money, but proudly clutching their own old toys.

Alongside the Advent Clear-Out is a clear-out of our souls. While you sort toys, talk about aspects of your own life you would like to see the back of. When choosing items that are good enough to give away praise your child for keeping the toy in a useable condition.

Make clear-out day the day your child vows to give up lying, answering back, pulling her sister's hair or cheating at cards. When you are planning to have family round at Christmas, you probably indulge in a bit of extra housework. This can help your child see that just as we make people feel welcome by tidying up first, so can we start the process of welcoming Christ into our own hearts by clearing out the ugly stuff.

Do-it-yourself Bethlehem

Deal with impatience for Christmas by creating a DIY Bethlehem using a nativity scene with figures, some Blu-tack and some figures drawn by the children or – if they are reluctant – by you. By moving the figures around the wall towards a 'stable', you can get the children to focus on the events which preceded Christmas, which are interesting in their own right.

Week One: First set up the stable at the beginning of Advent, in a safe place on one side of your living room. If you don't have a free-standing nativity set, try using a shoebox on its side painted brown. For added realism stuff in some hay from the pet-shop. If you prefer, use a picture of the Nativity or of the baby Jesus. Then over the next few days get your children to draw, on some stiff-ish card (e.g. cut from last year's Christmas cards):

✦ Mary
✦ Angel
✦ Elizabeth (pregnant)
✦ Zechariah
✦ Elizabeth
✦ baby John

Using the Blu-tack fix your figures to the living room, as far away as possible from the stable. Read together Luke 1:5–80 and let the children act out the series of encounters there:

✦ Zechariah and the angel
✦ Mary and the angel
✦ Elizabeth and Mary
✦ the birth of John

What would it be like to talk to an angel? Do you think it was hard for Mary to believe the angel? How did Mary show her faith in God?

Week Two: This week, read Luke 1:39–55. Talk about how Mary might have felt when she saw that her cousin Elizabeth was pregnant, just as the angel said she would be. Talk about times when you've needed 'proof' that God would keep his promises to your family. To end your devotions, read Mary's prayer (verses 46–55) together as your family's prayer of thanks and praise to God.

This is also time to draw and cut out Joseph. Move him and Mary round the wall, closer to the stable each time. Read Luke 2:1–4 together. Don't go on to the birth of Jesus – save that up.

Week Three: Now it is the turn of the Wise Men. Let imagination run riot in creating them, and don't forget to create a really nasty King Herod as well. Let them all be blu-tacked up, again, somewhere a good distance from the stable. Cut a large star out of gold paper and blu-tack that above them; move it nearer the stable each time you move it. Talk about exciting or difficult journeys you have made in the past; compare your worst holiday trip with the journey of the Magi. Talk about how the Wise Men are looking for Jesus – it is difficult but they have a star to guide them. What guides us in finding Jesus?

Read Matthew 2:2–12 together. Save the bit about the Holy Family's escape to Egypt until after Christmas.

Week Four: 'Father Christmas is a lovely fantasy, but the nativity story is real,' says Diana, a mother of four who, with help from her two teenagers, sets up an elaborate nativity scene on her front lawn in South London every year. No winking or waving Father Christmases for this family; the parents and children work hard to erect a life-like stable to the delight and wonder of neighbours.

The more real you can make the Christmas story, the better. At some point amid the pre-Christmas rush, get the card and scissors out again and fix up some shepherds, lambs and perhaps some more angels; read Luke 2:8–20. Talk about the shepherds, the difficult and dangerous work they had to do.

How do you think the shepherds felt when they heard the angel calling to them? The shepherds told lots of people about what happened. Do you think people believed them? How do you feel when you tell people about Jesus? End your time by asking God to help you tell other people about Jesus.

By about Christmas Eve all these figures should be nearing the stable. If you have free-standing crib figures, now is the time to get them out and set up Mary and Joseph and the animals in the stable. For very small children, have a conversation about the child's own bed. Talk about how soft and warm it is. Then ask your child to think about Jesus' bed in the manger. What did Jesus' bed feel like?

Talk about babies. How is a baby different from a king? Would people expect God's Son to come to earth as a little baby? If you don't have a full-scale crib set up, help your child make a little bed in a shoebox with some pet shop hay, to help visualise Jesus' first bed.

For older children

Watching the way people talk about Christmas

When non-Christians talk about 'the spirit of Christmas', or complain that an ungenerous or cruel act is 'especially bad, coming at Christmas', they are, sometimes without even realising it, talking about specifically *Christian* values. They may even be vaguely aware that Christ has asked us to give to the poor, to think of the lonely, the sick and the unwanted.

Of course Christ does not ask us to love our neighbours for one week of the year (or even just for the two-month Christmas shopping period!) He wants us to follow him all year round. But it is fascinating at Christmas-time to see how people with no room in their lives for Christ have nonetheless picked up some of his commands and stashed them away in their moral junk room in a box marked 'For Christmas only'.

Try asking an older child or teenager to keep their eyes and ears open for statements — on the television news, perhaps, or in newspapers — suggesting that some misfortune is 'especially sad at Christmas'. Ask your children why they think this assumption is made by the speaker. Ask: 'Where do people get the idea that Christmas should be a happy time?' 'Why does the speaker think that we should be kinder to each other, especially to people worse off than ourselves, at Christmas than at other times?'

Your aim is to help your child to see for himself or herself how Christianity, far from being marginalised or irrelevant, is in fact embedded so deeply in our culture that most people are not even aware of it. This is true 'preparation for Christmas' — the task of opening your child's eyes to the amazing, simple truth of God's incarnation as Jesus.

What Can I Give Him?...

Whichever church you belong to, the theme of Advent is one of preparation. We prepare ourselves to greet the Lord; we ask forgiveness for our sins, we try to think of spiritual gifts we can bring to the baby Jesus.

Involve your children in this process by talking about ways in which they can give Jesus a spiritual present — invoke Christina

Rossetti's beautiful lines, 'What can I give Him? Give my heart.'

Talk with your child about spiritual gifts for Jesus: not material objects, not money, but acts of kindness, prayers and acts of worship.

Here's one thing that you can do, and the only equipment you need is one of those old-fashioned Advent calendars – the sort with little pictures behind windows. Children under the age of about nine are charmed by the idea of opening a window each day. Choose an Advent calendar with a Nativity scene on it, if possible. Steer clear of the ones with chocolate inside. I don't say this out of meanness. For children, the joy of expectation can be very powerful, but it is a joy that has to be learnt.

One of the best Christmas gifts you can give your children is the art of learning to wait for Christmas. An ability to enjoy the idea of pleasures to come – as opposed to feeling miserable unless those pleasures are provided here and now – has been identified as one of the common characteristics of habitually happy people. Think back to your own childhood: the chances are that it is the sense of eagerness in the weeks before Christmas that made it magical. A few ounces less of chocolate before Christmas never hurt any child, and absence of chocolate-munching will also help you to focus the child's mind on the real meaning of Advent and the calendar.

Start Advent by writing 'Baby Jesus' Christmas list' on a piece of paper stuck to the calendar (that way you will be reminded of it every time one of the windows is opened). Encourage the child to think up some ideas of good, kind or helpful things that would make good 'Christmas presents' for Jesus.

At first, and particularly with small children, stick to specific little tasks, which are easier for the child to identify such as 'help load the dishwasher', 'read a story with my little sister', 'Go with Mum to visit the old lady down the road who is living on her own'. Include acts of prayer and commitments to go to church. Specific targets are easier to make a success of – and success is encouraging.

Later in the month or with older children add on more generalised 'Christmas presents', e.g. 'Share with my little sister' and more difficult negative intentions, e.g. 'Avoid being rude to Mum and Dad'. Write in new ideas whenever you or your child think of them.

Give my heart

The 'Christmas presents for Jesus' should never involve any financial outlay on the child's part. On the whole children have very little or no money and need to learn as much as possible about non-financial ways in which they can help and give.

While giving money is an important part of a Christian's duty, this Advent calendar is attempting to teach your child that money and money-values are not spiritual values. The Christmas presents for Jesus may develop into what are essentially New Year's Resolutions, which – as we all know – are always better kept if the resolver has thought about them for a few weeks before 1 January.

A sample Christmas present list for Jesus for a child aged seven

Jesus wants us to:	I will give Him:	I achieved it on:
think of others	helping my baby sister to play with her toys	12, 13 Dec 17, 19 Dec
	helping Mum clear up breakfast stuff	all first week! most of last week
look after the weak	remember to feed the cat	most of 2nd week!
stop quarrelling	no squabbling with brother all day	23 Dec (hooray)
pray to him	say prayers at night	every night!

Talk about how all through Advent, all the spiritual Christmas presents listed on your Christian Advent Calendar are stored up for the Baby Jesus. Talk about how Christ has shown us that the only true path for mankind is to heed His words all year round, not just at Christmas.

Every day, when the child opens one of the little windows, you have an opportunity to remind the child gently of their personal Christmas presents for Jesus and ask, 'Did you manage to store up a present yesterday? Do you think you will be able to do it today? Which of the ideas would you be able to use today?'

Write down the child's responses and ideas (use the back of the calendar or anything that won't get lost): on Christmas Eve put the list of 'Gifts for Jesus' next to your Christmas crib; or under the tree. Then on Christmas Day your child really will have something to give Jesus.

If doing this every day seems rather hard work at a busy time of year, just cut back to discussing it once a week and use the four-week structure of Advent to your advantage. Divide a sheet of paper into four sections and write in the child's Gifts for Jesus as they are achieved.

As your children grow older and start considering the idea of Gifts for Jesus too babyish, quietly stop making them write out lists, but go on talking about the basic concept. When discussing Christmas arrangements for socialising with your teenagers, or ideas for Christmas presents, slip in, 'And what about Jesus? What are you giving Him this year?'

It does of course help if you begin the conversation by telling your child what *your* Christmas present for Jesus is going to be. So think about it. Let the job of increasing your children's spirituality help your own to grow.

It is not easy to persuade older children or teenagers to participate in an exercise like this, especially if they are going through periods of doubt. Don't worry. If you persuaded them to plan their own presents for Jesus just once, they will one day remember that day with love. If you managed it two or three years in a row, the children will, as adults, look back on it as an age-old tradition handed down through your family (such is the rose-tinted power of childhood memories!) for generations, and may even one day start something of the same kind with their own children.

If Santa isn't real, what about Jesus?

The fatso in the red suit (to borrow a line from poet Matthew Sweeney) takes up a lot of space at Christmas, elbowing the baby in the manger into the shadows. In their thousands, Western children still write their letters to Santa and put them, unstamped and addressed to 'Father Christmas, North Pole, The World' into letter boxes. In the United Kingdom they are dealt with by the Post Office at a special department in Northern Ireland, and in the United States, a small band of volunteers living in the town of Santa Claus, South Georgia, carefully logs the letters from children.

Over the years, say the Santa Claus experts in both countries, the tone of children's letters has changed, in a surprising way. It is not simply that the items children ask for have changed: of course they ask for the latest must-have toy, and the simple doll or toy train has been replaced by the ubiquitous PlayStation or computer game.

No, the real change in children's letters to Santa is that children are now asking Santa Claus not for material goods, but for happiness: to 'bring Dad and Mum back together again' or 'find Dad a new job' or, very often, 'to please stop all the fighting and wars'. These are not traditional letters to Santa any more: *they are prayers*. Children are now asking Santa Claus to do what Christians have always been supposed to ask Jesus to do. No one knows the background of the children who ask Santa for better things to happen in their lives, but I would be willing to bet that most of them are from non-faith families. Feeling the need to pray, these children turn to the nearest thing to a deity that they know of: Santa Claus.

Intelligent parents have a dilemma over Santa Claus. He doesn't exist, right? Yet the myth of Santa is perpetuated in many families with more vigour than the story of Jesus' birth, certainly with more panache than the more important aspects of Christmas. Many families who never give a moment's thought to faith issues suddenly become very pious and whispery when the subject of Santa Claus comes up, because they believe it is important for their younger child to 'still believe' even though the older child has long since worked out the plot.

Children need a belief of some sort: if you give them nothing more substantial to believe in, they end up believing very earnestly in Santa Claus. Sadly, unlike Jesus, Santa has pretty poor theological back-up, for all that he is supposed to have started out as a bishop who rescued children from slavery and prostitution. The Churches can produce a good case for Jesus when the doubts start creeping in: but when your child stops believing your stories about Santa Claus, you look like a fraud; and your child begins to ask, 'What else that my parents have told me is true, is in fact totally untrue?' One Christian mother told me:

> My husband would like to banish Father Christmas, as part of the materialism of the whole Christmas shebang, but I don't think there is any need to get too fussed about Santa. He is part of growing up. The whole Santa thing has to be done light-heartedly, with a smile on your face, very tongue in cheek. My six-year-old has just begun to suspect he isn't true: OK, I said. But he might come just once more this year. The children don't want to believe it's not true; but because he doesn't exist I am not going to force them to believe in him. And not believing in Santa, as far as I am concerned, doesn't mean they won't get stockings.

Another mother of two says:

> We are pretty shameless about carrying on the Father Christmas myth – it is fun, after all. There is an inbetween area between believing and not believing which children

inhabit comfortably, and Father Christmas lives in that grey area.

A mother of four observes:

> Santa comes into the conversation in a jokey way that real-
> ly is far removed from the way we talk about God. We never
> make a big deal of hiding the truth – why should we? My
> first principle with my children is that I should never, never
> lie to them – they would always find me out.

Making Christmas Real

Try to encourage an awareness that the Christmas story actually happened, even though expert opinion varies on the details. Talk to your child about what it would have been like to be Mary and Joseph. How do you think Mary and Joseph felt about being in a strange town and having nowhere to sleep? When have you felt scared or alone? Was it hard for you to trust God during that time?

We all love infant school nativity plays, especially when something goes wrong and the innkeeper, in tea-towel and pencilled-in goatee beard, cheerfully invites Joseph and Mary to use his best honeymoon suite instead of the stable in the script. Actually, I would go further than that and say that I know some parents who would probably admit they had children specifically to enable them to go to infant nativity plays and have a good cry.

There is one tiny snag with infant school nativity plays: it is that they are performed by infants. Very adorable, but regular annual exposure serves not so much to bring the Christmas story home to us as to distance it. The infant nativity play represents the troubled older man who was Joseph, and the strangely assured young woman facing the dangers of childbirth in a cave who was Mary as chubby six-year-olds with towels on their heads, cutely searching the audience for their mums and dads and lovably fluffing their lines. The underlying effect is to turn the story into a nursery tale, suitable only for acting out by under-eights.

So while the nativity play is a wonderful tradition, and important for clarifying the story for small children, older children and adults need to be able to grow away from the nursery and read the story as though it happened, and happened to real grown-ups, not to six-year-olds raiding the dressing up box.

Nativity plays with adults playing the major roles are rare indeed. One such takes place annually in the Surrey village of Wintershall. One Christian mother who has taken her two teenagers and two young adopted children twice describes it as

> ... brilliant. There are adults dressed up as Mary and Jesus, not school pantomime stuff. It is so real for the children. You go there in the dark, you climb up a hill to find the shepherds guarding the sheep by firelight, then the Angel appears in the top of a tree. It's not all Christmas tinsel by any means: there's King Herod; the massacre of the Holy Innocents; the children find themselves close up to the nasty soldiers; it's real good against evil, quite scary.

The production uses live cattle, sheep and goats alongside the actors. Staged in an eighteenth-century barn on the 1100-acre Wintershall estate in Bramley, Surrey, it draws a five-thousand-strong audience. For more information see the resources section.

Joy and Hope

Now that Christmas is so heavily secularized, what exactly has it lost, and what has it gained? It has certainly gained status as a time when we feel emboldened to hold out hands of friendship to people of other faiths and of none. The best aspect of the modern Christmas must surely be its universality – the ease with which everyone feels drawn together.

And the loss? It has slipped into being a mere celebration of cheerfulness, a time of relaxation that contrives never to be particularly relaxing. Cheerfulness and relaxation are all very well, but they cannot do the same work as joy and hope.

Joy is a deeper, more spiritual emotion; it wells up through sorrow, through bereavement, through disappointment. If you can fix your children's minds on the joy of a baby's birth and the pleasure of giving rather than receiving, then they can begin to grow into a more meaningful sense of Christmas.

Hope is the knowledge that whatever happens, we are loved and capable of loving back. It is what carries people through terrible Christmasses — those spent in hardship, at times of unemployment, sickness, homelessness, bereavement. Hope and joy, not cheerfulness and relaxation, are the feelings which make intolerable Christmasses tolerable. So let joy and hope, rather than cheerfulness and relaxation, be at the heart of your Christmas. Oh — and have a merry one!

'... they can walk past shop windows without feeling the painful tug of "the gimmes".'

5

Forty days of fasting and prayer! What an extraordinary idea Lent is, and how completely impossible to fit into a twenty-first century life of instant gratification and constant snacks. And what a strange idea to stick it in what should be the most beautiful part of the year, the spring. I

Cutting Out the Extras and Believing in Miracles: Lent and Easter

say *should* be, because for all the skipping lambs and bursting blossom, spring is not half as interesting to children as Christmas or the summer holidays.

But what a good place to put something special. The cornucopia and excitement of Christmas are far behind, the glories of summer activities and holidays, or the tensions of summer exams, are still far ahead. On the whole, spring is definitely boring. If you doubt me, ask a passing child.

One of the nicest things about putting faith into your family life is that you gain a structure to your calendar. Once you become aware of the Christian year, you have a whole bunch of little landmarks in your diary to look forward to. These landmarks are a tremendous help if you are at home with small children and looking for something to differentiate one day of play-group–lunch–park–home from another. They

are also a great boon if your older children need lots of encour-
agement in meeting targets of any kind – behaviour, school
work, music practice. Children respond very readily to the idea
of different seasons having their own special qualities. You can
tell that just by watching the delight they take in the trappings
of Christmas.

The challenges of Lent make what might otherwise be a
rather boring 'middle stretch' of the school year potentially
interesting – a time when we set new goals, set ourselves
challenges in the form of small acts of self-denial, or try to get
better at praying. It is especially a time of prayer, and introducing Lent prayers into daily life gives this season its own
flavour. For me Lent is conveniently placed just where I need it,
when my New Year's resolutions have crashed and I still fondly
and usually erroneously believe I have plenty of time left to
make the year a Good Year.

Like Advent, Lent seems to be exactly the right length for a
family spiritual exercise, long enough to give a busy parent time
for a false start before getting back on track, but short enough to
allow full concentration on an intense burst of activity. And
above all, Lent is about simplifying your life – spring-cleaning it
and de-cluttering it, identifying the things you need and the
things it won't hurt to do without for a few weeks.

Of course, for most Britons Lent does not exist. It does not
exist for many of the majority who consider themselves 'spiritual
people' simply because many of them are not Christians: but
neither does it exist for those who consider themselves nominally
Christians. This was sharply brought home to me when I heard
a supposedly learned celebrity quiz show contestant confidently
assert, with the cheerful agreement of the quizmaster, that
Shrove Tuesday 'celebrates the end of Lent'. (It doesn't. It marks
the beginning of Lent.)

So if you would like to explore Lent with your children this
year, you will need to start with the story of Jesus in the desert,
found in Matthew 4:1–11, Mark 1:12–13 and Luke 4:1–13.

Before he gathered his disciples and began his short but intense ministry, Jesus fasted for forty days and nights in the desert, wrestling with some interesting temptations put in front of him by Satan, who was trying to encourage Jesus to misuse his powers. We remember this period of preparation during the six weeks before Easter; we pray extra hard and we try to make special sacrifices to show that we mean to follow Jesus. What does this mean for children?

Beating the 'Gimmes'

'Why is Adam crying?' one of our children asked a school friend one day. 'Oh, his parents said he would be getting a Sony PlayStation 2 this week but the shop had run out,' explained his friend.

It is no picnic being a toy-fashion victim. Children who cannot walk past a toyshop or a branch of Dixons without bursting into a tirade of 'I want's' are quite obviously not happy children. They are torturing themselves with desires. The boy who burst into tears because the Sony PlayStation 2 he had been promised would arrive *that week* had not turned up was not behaving like a happy child. Believing quite genuinely that his happiness depended on a piece of technology made him very vulnerable.

Teaching our children to do without the things they crave – at least for a while – is nothing more nor less than teaching them to *be happy*. It is liberating to discover that happiness is not permanently increased by another computer game, another designer T-shirt or another CD. If you encourage children to give up a consumer pleasure during Lent then you are training them to live happily in the consumer world and helping them towards the day when they can walk past shop windows without feeling the painful tug of the 'gimmes'.

Lenten sacrifices do not have to be food, and in fact it is not a bad idea to play down the giving-up of favourite foods. Giving up chocolate, chips or whatever smacks too much of ordinary slimming routines and so can confuse children as to what Lent is about. Lent is a time of prayer, not a time of slimming down to fit into the holiday swimsuit.

The Busy Family's Forty-day Lent Plan

A series of wonderful forty-day plans for Lent can be found on an American website, www.simpleliving.org, which belongs to a pressure group dedicated to reducing the materialism of Christmas and other Christian festivals. I love the way their Lenten plans, revised every year with different themes and twists, stress that Lent is a time for de-cluttering your life, and I like the way they emphasise 'non-monetary' forms of giving which are easier for children, who have little money, to achieve. And the activities which are designed to heighten awareness of the resources of the earth might, just *might* make Lent a little bit more cool in the eyes of your cynical teenager.

I have adapted some of the simpleliving.org ideas here specifically for families with school-age children. The Bible readings are from one cycle of readings in the Church calendar: there are other cycles which you may wish to explore later when you have got to grips with the idea. Some of the activities require you to put aside a 'token' – a promise to give a small agreed amount to charity. You could fix a tariff of £1 for an adult, 20p for a child, 50p for an older child or teenager, or £5 for the whole household together. Put the tokens in a collecting tin, either as coins or pieces of scrap paper with 'promises' written on them.

Ash Wednesday. Read Matthew 6:1: 'Beware of practising your piety before others in order to be seen by them; for then you have no reward from your father in heaven.' Children understand this idea almost better than adults. For children it means 'Don't boast to all your friends about being good!' The idea is especially important to us today because in a multi-cultural school or community, it is not good manners to parade your Christianity.

But on the other hand, if people ask you about your Lenten practices out of genuine curiosity, tell them what you can and don't be ashamed of it. Catholics go to a special Ash Wednesday service where the minister makes a cross with ashes on each person's forehead. After I have been marked in this way, I can never stop myself wondering whether I should wipe it off afterwards. Half of me feels I am parading the fact that I have been to church that day. Half of me wants to be a living reminder to the people around me of the meaning of Ash Wednesday; and when the woman behind the counter at the newsagent's says kindly, 'Excuse me, Madam, but you've got a smudge of dirt on your forehead,' it doesn't hurt either of us for me briefly to explain how it got there.

Thursday. If you normally go to school, nursery or playgroup by car, walk or take public transport just for today and to-morrow. If that's impossible, then keep the car radio turned off during the journey for two days, and cut down your car journeys this week. Spend the time talking about how much of the world's precious resources we could save by cutting out pointless journeys. Give thanks to God for our world's resources and promise to use them more wisely.

Friday or St Valentine's Day (14 February). St Valentine is the patron saint not only of lovers but of prisons, prisoners and their staff. Say a prayer for prisoners and their families waiting for them to be released; say a prayer for those who work in prisons. Say a prayer for prison chaplains. Swap this activity with whichever activity falls on 14 February this year.

Saturday. Think about Jesus' self-denial in the desert. Plan some little acts of self-denial for yourselves. Get the children to come up with their own ideas. Help them to keep their goals realistic – 'eating chips only once a week' rather than 'giving up chips completely'.

First Sunday in Lent. Read Matthew 4:1–11. Think about all the children in the world who don't have enough to eat. Over thirty thousand children die every day from hunger-related causes. Get children to identify a non-essential but regularly consumed 'goodie' (the break-time biscuit or soft drink, the after-school packet of crisps etc.) that they could occasionally forego, and suggest that you will put a token in the token jar for each time they do without.

Monday. Try this magic trick: use only *half* of the usual amount of toothpaste that you normally use. The tube magically becomes twice as big! Can you think of things you could use *half* of once or twice a week?

Tuesday. Find a globe or a map of the world. Find where your home is. Take some time to look at the globe or map and talk about it — which areas are most thickly populated, where you went on holiday last year, where Aunt Ethel emigrated to — whatever takes your fancy. Then encourage your child/children to think about how this world is entrusted to us by God. Say a prayer for the world.

Wednesday. On the way home from school talk about things you have bought in the past which you did not really need. Get everyone to think of a toy or other possession that they thought they wanted but which was hardly used once it had been obtained. If you still have the toy, give it away to a charity shop, toy library or hospital.

Thursday. During his forty days in the wilderness, Jesus was tempted to misuse his powers for his own pleasure and comfort. Today, think about each person in the family's special gifts or talents. If you have time, write them down. Think about how tempting it is to use our special gifts just for our own satisfaction and gain.

Friday. More thoughts about *power*. Parents have power over children: do you ever misuse it? Siblings, especially older siblings, have the power to make their brothers' or sisters' lives happy or miserable. Ask your children to think of times they may have misused their power. Put a token in the collecting tin for each episode that they remember.

Saturday. Listening Day. Sometimes it is hard to hear God's voice. Read the story of Elijah in 1 Kings 19:11–12:

> Now there was a great wind, so strong that it was splitting mountains and breaking rocks in pieces before the LORD, but the LORD was not in the wind; and after the wind an earthquake, but the LORD was not in the earthquake; and after the earthquake a fire, but the LORD was not in the fire; and after the fire a sound of sheer silence. When Elijah heard it, he wrapped his face in his mantle and went out and stood at the entrance of the cave. Then there came a voice to him that said, 'What are you doing here, Elijah?'

See if you can spend fifteen minutes in silence together, praying and listening for God's voice. If this is impossible for your children, cut it down to five minutes.

Second Sunday in Lent. Read John 3:1–17. Think about the mysterious idea of being 'born again'. The people Jesus was talking with clearly thought it was nonsense at first. But Jesus' words refer to something other than physical birth. The idea of reaching a different level of awareness through spiritual and mental exercise is universally accepted. When a baby is born it looks at the world with new eyes; everything is new and fresh. People who live in faith, prayer and devotion often describe a feeling of newness descending on them: as one very holy man put it to me, 'the feeling of old lenses being cast off and new ones fitted'.

Monday. Try the magic 'halving' trick again — this week apply it to convenience foods or junk food and drinks. You might even have started to lose an unwanted pound or two by now!

Tuesday. Water Day. While water covers three-quarters of the earth's surface, 97.4 per cent is salt water; 1.8 per cent is frozen; only 0.8 per cent is fresh water. Say a prayer of thanks before you use water in the shower, the bath or the washbasin and try not to waste any.

Wednesday. Whose is the next birthday you need to buy a present for? Consider buying something for them today, not in the regular shops but in a charity shop which will use the proceeds to benefit Third World families starting their own businesses.

Thursday. Go outdoors more today, even if it is raining. Pay attention to what is going on around you — can you feel spring?

Friday. No Wasted Food Day. Make a resolution that today not one scrap of edible food is going to end up in the waste bin, even if it means serving smaller portions.

Saturday. Here is a prayer that harks back to the difficult theme of last Sunday:

> O God, Giver of life and light, call us from our wombs of security and isolation to rebirth into the world you are creating; call us from the darkness of our fears and anxieties to the daytime of hope and confidence in your ministry. Amen.

Third Sunday in Lent. Is there anyone in our lives whom we avoid in the way that Jesus' contemporaries shunned the Samaritans? Is there a child in the school playground who has no friends? Get your children at least to think about befriending a lonely or unliked child during the coming week.

Monday. The 'halving' game focuses this week on cutting down critical remarks to each other. Think twice before making a negative remark — and try to make a positive comment instead!

Tuesday. Water Day again. 'The average African woman has to carry water for four hours each day.' Put two tokens in your collecting tin for every glass of water you drink today. Read the story of Jesus and the Samaritan woman in John 4:6–14. What does Jesus mean by 'living water'?

Wednesday. Smile. Say hello especially warmly to everyone you meet! Oh, all right then, just the people you know already.

Thursday. 'You shall not covet . . . anything that belongs to your neighbour.' Yet coveting seems to have become a way of life for many people. Instead of coveting, look around you for things you really don't need.

Friday. Find out something about an ethnic group different from your own.

Saturday. Read Psalm 95 — it is full of joy and thanks for creation.

Fourth Sunday in Lent. Read John 9, the story of the man Jesus cured of blindness and the refusal of the Pharisees to 'see' where Jesus came from. Sometimes we do not see the wood for the trees; sometimes we do not see the answer when it is staring us in the face. Ask the children — have you ever been searching for something only to find it right in front of your eyes?

Monday. Jesus technically broke the law to heal the blind man on the Sabbath. Talk with your children about when it might be right to break a rule. You will have an interesting discussion. Remove prized and fragile ornaments from view first. . .

Tuesday. Use the washing-up and bath water to water plants or flush the loo. It works just as well and saves lots of water.

Wednesday. No-packaging day. Get all the packaging your family threw away today. Weigh it on the bathroom scales and multiply by 365 to discover the approximate weight of packaging you throw away a year. Are there any ways you can reduce this amount that you have not explored already?

Thursday. The Pharisees were looking out for any evidence they could use to condemn Jesus: ask your family if there are times when they have looked for evidence to pile up against someone they just did not like.

Friday. Don't switch on the television today. Enjoy real life.

Saturday. Ask the children to pray with you while you are shopping:

> God of mystery, please help me decide if I really need this item or if I should save the money, or give it to someone who needs it more than we do. In Jesus' name, Amen.

Fifth Sunday in Lent. Read John 11:1–45, the story of the raising of Lazarus.

Monday. The 'halving' trick this week focuses on wasteful habits. Cut down the time the thermostat is on high; switch off lights; turn off the taps while brushing teeth. Get the children to be in charge of these.

Tuesday. It takes 2,500 gallons of water to produce one pound of beef. Plan today's meals without meat. When you do eat meat, pray a special prayer thanking God for the animals around us.

Wednesday. Think about planting a tree in your family's name through a charity such as the Woodland Trust (www.woodland-trust.org.uk).

Thursday. Can you give someone a gift today that is neither money nor an object bought with money? Adults can take trouble to give an ear to someone's troubles or be particularly patient with a child; children can offer to help a classmate struggling with schoolwork, or support someone being picked on in the playground.

Friday. Did you stick up for anyone who was suffering in the last year? Did it make you more vulnerable? Ask the children to remember times when they could have supported someone but decided not to because of the risk to themselves.

Saturday. Tomorrow is Palm Sunday. But discipleship means more than waving palms. Say the Lord's Prayer with your children today.

Palm/Passion Sunday. The people laid down their garments for Jesus to walk on. Think about things we are proud of that we might 'lay down' for Jesus.

Monday. Mary anointed Jesus' feet with costly perfume. Is there something valuable to you that you could honour Jesus with – by using it to help others, perhaps?

Tuesday. Put a luxury aside and do without it today.

Wednesday. Read one of the accounts of the last days of Jesus' earthly life in the Gospels in preparation for Easter.

Thursday. Today we remember the Last Supper, Jesus' last meal with his disciples. English kings used to wash the feet of the poor on this day; this evening wash each other's hands gently as a service to each other.

Good Friday. Read the story of Good Friday. 'If Jesus Christ were to come today, people would not even crucify him. They would ask him to dinner, and hear what he had to say, and make fun of it.' How is Jesus crucified today?

Saturday. Think about violence; if your children tend to squabble, challenge them to get through the day without a fight.

Easter Sunday. Read Luke 24:13–49; or put copies of the story of the Resurrection inside the packaging of the children's Easter eggs.

Easter: Believing in Miracles

The secular Christmas at least has an earthy, pagan point to it. The secular Easter is a festival so cut from its roots it is absurd. There cannot be anything more dispiriting than the act of exchanging Easter eggs made of chocolate when you have not observed any kind of self-denial for Lent, or than wishing each other a 'Happy Easter' without any awareness of its meaning.

If yours is the kind of child who likes making things, try your hand together at an Easter Garden. All you need is a tea tray, some moss, perhaps a bit of turf, and something to make a raised 'tomb' – Lego bricks are as serviceable as anything else especially if covered over with moss.

Remember the Wintershall Nativity Play I mentioned in chapter 4? The same group has performed a now celebrated Life of Christ at Eastertide. The grand scale of the occasion, moving the action around five different parts of the Wintershall estate, and the reality of the presentation make a huge impression on people of all ages. The action begins right at the beginning, with the Angel visiting the Virgin Mary before she had conceived the Son of God and a subsequent Nativity scene followed by scenes from Jesus' boyhood.

The audience is then herded off to another part of the

Wintershall estate for a potted version of Christ's ministry, beginning with the calling of the 'very ordinary' disciples. The action incorporates vivid retellings and dramatisations of parables and moves through miracles including the feeding of the five thousand – the number, incidentally, of a maximum capacity audience at Wintershall. The disciples involve the audience by bringing round bread for them to eat.

The climax of the day begins with the journey into Jerusalem on Palm Sunday, with the actors passing among the audience to greet Jesus; then the drama of Christ's Passion unfolds. One visitor from a distant parish wrote of her day at Wintershall: 'We came home emotionally drained, tired, but just so blessed by what we had seen.' A teenager wrote: 'The actor playing Jesus came up into the crowd and talked to us as if we were his followers. When he told a story, he asked all of the children to come down and sit around him.'

Ask local churches ahead of time if there is any Easter activity or pilgrimage you and your family could join, such as the Celebrate convention which takes place annually in the West Country, organised by young Catholics. If classical music is more your thing, look in the paper for performances of Bach's *St Matthew Passion* or *St John Passion*. Taking older children to an event such as this helps to make Easter more alive for them.

We cannot all go to wonderful Wintershall, alas. But peeling off the layers of tradition from the Easter story is something we have to keep doing, year after year. Young children have a remarkable knack of breaking through layers of tradition and looking at the story with completely new eyes and sometimes their simple belief can be very inspiring.

Many Christian parents I have talked to find their children's ability simply to believe in the Resurrection a spur for their own faith. The closest my children have got to the Wintershall experience is the lovely animated feature film *The Miracle Maker* which blends superb model animation with the voice skills of stars such as Ralph Fiennes, Miranda Richardson, David Thewlis and many others. The first time my youngest child saw this film she was three years old. Being only three, she took the whole story as a narrative on a level with any Disney movie. She scowled at Pontius Pilate; she burst into tears when Christ was crucified; and when Mary met the risen Christ at the tomb, she leapt from her seat and flung her arms round my neck with an overjoyed 'He's alive! He's alive!'

There was nothing else to say.

'... saying Grace ... in a a public eating place ...'

6

Some mothers feel it as quasi-sexual. 'Every time I walk into the sitting room,' complained the husband of a friend of mine to his wife soon after the birth of their baby, 'you two are snogging on the sofa.' Food is love, as every mother knows

For What We Are About to Receive

from the minute her eyes meet the calmly interested, yet adoring upward gaze of her suckling baby. The love in that gaze is the most intense love imaginable.

Snogging, indeed – something physical and close, breaking taboos against body contact. Something rather exciting, radical, forbidden. Children who have never seen a baby suckling get very giggly and squeal at the very idea. Many adults are uncomfortable with it too. We are so used to food coming well-labelled in vacuum-packed packages that the thought of nourishing an infant with stuff from one's own body is a bit *disgusting*, even when we know rationally that the stuff is very good for the baby.

But ask a new mother, maybe a week or so after the birth of her first baby, preferably when her milk is coming in properly, preferably when she has finally worked out how to hold the baby without getting sore nipples or a backache, and perhaps when she is starting to catch up on sleep a bit, if she finds it *disgusting* to be nourishing the one she loves with her own body, and you will get a wet nappy thrown at you. Such a mother is feeling a new depth of love she has never known, in giving and in receiving. And if she can feel that new depth of love, she has to admit to herself the possibility that there might exist further depths of love that none of us really know about. And if she is open to that idea, then suddenly the idea of divine love does not look so screwy after all.

Just as Christianity acknowledges the inexpressible wonder we feel at the bond between a mother and her child, so does it acknowledge in the most extraordinary way our deep instinct to show love with nourishment. Our basic 'food is love' instinct is translated onto a mystical plane in the Eucharist, the rite in which Christians eat bread or a form of it (for Westerners the 'bread' is usually a tasteless bit of white wafer very like cardboard) in memory of Jesus' last meal before he was crucified.

Now it has to be said that the idea of consuming the body of one's deity is just as, well, *disgusting* to modern sensibilities as the idea of breastfeeding is to many children, and the idea that saying some words over some dry wafers turns them into the body of the deity can seem perfectly ridiculous to rationalist non-Christians, and downright superstitious even to many mainstream Christians.

If you don't know the story behind the Christian rite of Holy Communion, also called the Eucharist, here it is in crude, brief detail. The night before he was crucified Jesus had a meal with his closest friends, the disciples. In accordance with the tradition they all knew well, he blessed a cup of wine and some bread; but in a new departure from tradition he told his companions that the bread and wine were his body and blood, adding, 'do this in remembrance of me'. You can read the story in Luke 22, especially verses 7–20.

One of the stories about Jesus after he rose from the dead is the story of his appearance to two of his close followers walking from Jerusalem to a village called Emmaus (Luke 24:13–35). The story goes that a stranger appeared to these two men, talked significantly with them about Jesus' death and then sat down to share a meal with them: when he 'took bread, blessed and broke it and gave it to them' the pairs' 'eyes were opened and the recognised him' at which point he 'vanished from their sight'. So this ritual was cemented into the Christian faith and for most Christians it is still an important way in which God is with us.

Food was central to two of Jesus' miracles and crops up throughout the Gospel story with a heart-warming regularity that adds to the sense of it being a real story, not a symbolic one.

Food and meals play a great role in Judaic rituals, and in Christianity its role is taken a step further, where the idea of God being physically present in the Eucharist calls up some very deep feelings in us which are akin to those we have when we are new parents. The closeness, the physical quality of words like *bread* and *eating*, the taboo-breaking aspect of eating the deity – do these not conjure up the same awful thrill which breastfeeding inspires?

As our children grow older, food continues to represent love. We are lucky enough in this country not to need to worry about whether our children will have enough to eat. Most of us are aware that More Food does not necessarily equal More Love, so our need to show love through food emerges in other ways.

We worry about children not eating the right food, or not enough, or too much. We worry if food that used to be considered safe is really poisonous to our children. We find out about allergies and reactions and pass alarming stories around from parent to parent. In whatever abundance it is available, food continues to be a channel for our love.

The mistake we usually make is in failing to carry through the glorious feelings of early parenthood into later life. If feeding your baby was a mystical experience, why not let feeding your growing family have a mystical aspect?

The Family Dinner Table

We are always being told that families 'don't eat together any more'. I am sceptical of this because I find the alternative scenario rather too much like hard work. Compared with providing an endless series of little snack meals and convenience foods, it really is easier, quicker and more economical to offer one meal to everyone in the family, and to insist that they eat it at the same time, in the same place. Whether the one meal in question is from the microwave or not strikes me as rather unimportant.

Eating together as a family does not necessarily mean eating roast beef and Yorkshire pudding with onion gravy. You could be eating a packet of crisps each – the main thing is that you share and eat together.

If you are one of those families which eats together regularly, you will know what a maelstrom of feeling the family dinner table can be. Whether it be happiness, hilarity, misery or rage, whatever feelings happen to be flying around the house seem to be drawn to the dining table at 6.00 p.m. (or whenever your usual mealtime is supposed to be) like clouds of dust to the centre of a tornado. There are times, frankly, when I wish that a tornado would just pick me up, fling me over the rainbow and set me down in the land of the Munchkins, or anywhere peaceful where people don't call each other awful names all the time.

Brave the tornado – keep up with the family meal. It really is worth it. At the very worst times, it is a chance to take stock of your family, notice who needs a haircut, who is going through a fit of sulks that might be a sign of trouble at school, whose table manners need brushing up. It is a chance to check up on what is going on in everyone's lives.

At the best times, it is a joy. My family usually finds itself eating together at lunchtime at weekends. It is not always very nice. But every now and again we reach the end of a Saturday or Sunday lunch during which child A has told a funny joke, child

B has informed us of a major triumph at school, and everyone has eaten what was on their plates *and* cleared their own place, thus winning oodles of adoration from their pitifully easily-pleased mother. At times like these the sun comes out with its hat on and no mistake. And if we have managed to pause at some point in our meal to allow God's voice to speak within us, then the magic glow is unsurpassed and we feel we have given our children a wonderful memory to carry through their lives. So go for it.

Saying grace

Judith, mother of three, remembers:

> I was out for the day with a friend and our two four-year-old daughters. We were both at a very God-aware state in our lives – I was an ex-atheist approaching baptism, my friend a lapsed Catholic returning enthusiastically to the bosom of the church. So we were both pretty enthusiastic about all things prayer-related, right?
>
> The four of us sat down in a café for lunch and immediately one of the little girls asked the other, 'Shall we say *your* grace, Emily?' The other one said, 'No, let's say *your* grace, I like it better.'
>
> 'Hang on,' my friend and I both said, hastily. 'We can't say grace in a *restaurant!*'
>
> The children rounded on us: '*Why not?*' they chorused. Both adults crumbled – we just couldn't think of a good excuse not to say grace. So the girls proceeded – and of course we had to have *both* graces … one of which was in Latin. The entire café fell totally silent and my friend and I were beetroot with embarrassment.
>
> But nothing happened to us. We came out of it alive. It wasn't such a big deal. And now we always say grace in public places. My husband – who used to be very sniffy about any kind of public show of religion – actually now

says grace with me if we go out for a romantic dinner together.

My family and I also normally say grace at the beginning of the meal when we are all together. It guarantees peace, or at least cessation of hostilities, for about five seconds, for which I am grateful. It does not guarantee a peaceful meal. But it helps to remind us all that we are part of God's family and that as such we have standards to live up to. And if the children are too busy arguing about who has got the larger piece of chicken to think about that, then it helps to remind the parents, at least.

I have even seen it claimed that saying grace before a meal is good for your health. Since prayer is meant to be good for your health, saying grace must be doubly so: instead of grabbing your fork and digging in, you approach your food in a more relaxed, tranquil state of mind with less tension. Less tension means better digestion, which is generally good for your health.

In fact on the purely practical level for parents, saying grace gives a starting-point to the meal and helps to calm the children down if they have come in from some boisterous game or other. This is doubly true if you are in a public eating place – saying grace in a motorway café always has an interesting subduing effect on our children. Whether this effect is God's grace or freezing embarrassment, I am not sure.

If you have never said grace before at meals, do not expect it to be easy to start. You will feel self-conscious and theatrical. You will feel inhibited about saying grace in front of friends or other family members, such as your parents, if you were not brought up with the custom. As would-be Christian parents find time after time, the British sense of embarrassment, which is an excellent protective shield against fanaticism, can also work the other way, as an obstacle to freely-expressed faith and to any display that might possibly require audience participation.

Saying grace before meals certainly does not amount to a life of prayer, but it is a good place for the average inhibited Brit to start bringing spirituality out of the church and into the every-day world of your home. Ram Gidoomal, an Evangelical Christian activist and father of three who came to his faith from Hinduism, told me that once he and his family had got into the – to Ram's family – outlandish Christian habit of saying grace before meals, it eventually became – and this tends to happen with all the Christian customs if you give them a chance – something they could not manage a meal without.

Here's how to say grace at the beginning of a meal. Wait until everyone is sitting down and quiet. This is a good exercise for parents: the practice of getting your children to respond to a school-style 'quiet now' that comes from you rather than from a teacher. They may not respond very well at first – don't let that bother you. Persist.

Start with a simple formulaic grace like 'For what we are about to receive, may the Lord make us truly thankful, Amen.' Catholics then make the sign of the cross ('In the name of the Father, the Son and the Holy Spirit, Amen'); Protestants do not make the sign of the cross, and I suspect this has less to do with theological history and more to do with our old friend the British embarrassment factor.

The British embarrassment factor must also play a part in the popularity of jokey 'graces' which people sometimes teach small children: 'Rub a dub dub, thanks for the grub', 'Bless the bunch who munch this lunch', 'For Bacon, Eggs and Buttered Toast, Praise Father, Son and Holy Ghost' and so on. The justification is that such bits of doggerel break the ice, which is fine, but it is a shame if the joke grace is allowed to elbow more serious prayers completely out of the picture.

Some of us may be lucky enough to have grandparents or parents who can pass down a grace which they learned as children; other older people, if memories are gently jogged, might be able to repeat a grace learnt years ago even though they long since gave up saying it. Using this grace will give you a thread of continuity between generations. If your child is old enough, get him or her to ask a grandparent to recall the grace they 'used to' know.

If you don't have a family grace – or don't much fancy the one that you have inherited – try some of these. One idea which resonates with older children who are becoming more aware of injustice in the world is that not everyone in the world has enough to eat. A simple grace acts as a gentle reminder of this fact:

From the Book of Common Prayer:

> Give us grateful hearts, O Father, for all thy mercies, and make us mindful of the needs of others; through Jesus Christ our Lord. Amen.

A slightly more modern extension of the same:

> Bless, O Lord, this food to our use and us to thy loving service; and keep us ever mindful of the needs of others. Amen.

Even shorter:

> Bless this food to our use, and us to thy service, and make us ever mindful of the needs of others. Amen.

If you find 'this food to our use' ugly:

> For the bounty laid before us, may the Lord make us thankful, and ever mindful of the needs of others. Amen.

The idea of thinking of others who are less fortunate than ourselves is carried in many attractive graces, such as this Methodist grace:

> Lord God, we thank you for all the good things you provide, and we pray for the time when people everywhere shall have the abundance they need.

Here is a more ecologically aware grace:

Thank you, Lord, for this food which is set before us. May we use it to nourish our bodies, and thee to nourish our souls. Make us ever more mindful of the needs of others, and the needs of our planet. Through Christ our Lord, Amen.

This one hails from a Canadian aid charity:

For food in a world where many walk in hunger;
For faith in a world where many walk in fear;
For friends in a world where many walk alone;
We give you thanks, O Lord. Amen.

Thanking God for food is the main element of a grace. But this moment of shared prayer is also a good opportunity to thank God for each other's company as we eat together. Some graces also give a nod to those who prepare the food.

For good food and those who prepare it,
For good friends with whom to share it,
We thank you Lord. Amen.
              (by a Yorkshire Anglican clergyman, Peter Dunbar)

Here is a nice swingy grace that small children love learning, with hand actions that I have added to. The rhyming of 'the birds that sing' with 'everything' seems a little desperate and, if you happen to be eating poultry, downright tactless. But at least it avoids the awkward rhyming of 'good' with 'food' which so many composers of mealtime graces seem to favour:

Thank you for the food we eat,
(hold hands out in front, palms open, towards table)
Thank you for the friends we meet,
(hold hands out to sides towards others)
Thank you for the birds that sing,
(point to sky)
Thank you, God, for everything.
(make a big circle with your arms)

This one is very similar, if a little more elegant:

> Thank you God for the food we eat,
> Thank you God for the friends we meet,
> Thank you God for the sun above,
> *(hold hand up with palm extended)*
> Thank you God for your love.
> *(hand on heart)*
> Amen.

I particularly like graces which make a point of inviting Jesus to the table. It is wonderful to be reminded at an ordinary lunch time that he is there with us.

Here is a Lutheran one:

> Come, Lord Jesus, be our guest, and let these gifts to us be blessed. O give thanks unto the Lord for He is good, and His mercy endures forever. Amen.

More simply still:

> Come Lord Jesus be our guest, let this food to us be blessed.

This is a Spanish Catholic grace with a similar sentiment:

> *Cristo, pan de vida/ Ven y bendice esta comida. Amen.*
> Christ, bread of life/ Come and bless this food. Amen.

This one is also of Methodist origin, and is sometimes called the 'Wesley Grace'. It can be sung to the tune of *Praise God, from whom all blessings flow*, perhaps with everyone holding hands:

> Be present at our table, Lord!
> Be here and everywhere adored.
> Thy creatures bless, and grant that we
> May feast in Paradise with Thee! Amen.

The last line is enough to give anyone a good appetite and might even start the children off imagining what kind of food might be provided for feasting in Paradise with the Lord. If this image of the afterlife is too primitive for you, however, the last line can be changed to:

May strengthened for thy service be.

As you become more comfortable with saying grace, you can start occasionally introducing some fancy ritual touches which will enhance the atmosphere of the meal and make it special. Try lighting a candle in the middle of the table as you say grace, to remind everyone that Jesus is the Light of the World. Let the children take it in turns to blow the candle out at the end of the meal and ask Jesus to let his light shine in their lives through the day.

Some Christian families use the standard grace as an opportunity for free-form prayer, adding prayers for members of the family who are ill or have other trials in their lives; some children enjoy taking it in turns to think of something they wish to 'offer up' to God at that moment. Don't be put off if they are too inhibited at first.

Peaceful mealtimes

Putting Christianity into your daily routine with your children means creating happy, faith-filled memories for them that, as adults, they will want to re-create for their own children. Squabbling, chaotic mealtimes where the dinner table seems to become the eye of the storm do not make for happy memories.

I've gathered together some strategies for making mealtimes more pleasant. Many Christian families are well aware of how important the eating-together ritual is to their faith, and they try very hard to make it special. There are even board games to help you smooth things along at those times when you feel you are on the sibling rivalry front line. You may have heard of 'The Un-Game', a quiz game using cards with trivia questions that is successfully used by youth leaders to get teenagers talking and sharing opinions.

I have a similar thing – it is called just 'The family dinner game', and is distributed by the Family Caring Trust. Calling it a game is stretching a point but it was clearly invented by someone with a large and quarrelsome family. However, it is perfectly suitable for most family set-ups. It consists of six sets of cards on which are printed categories of thought: 'Likes and dislikes', 'I remember', 'I feel', 'Imagine', 'I value' and a Wild Card category.

Each person takes a turn to roll a dice and picks up a card to answer the question or complete a sentence on the back: 'A time I felt frightened or scared was…' or 'this is a story I heard about one of my grandparents' (if a child in the family is adopted or fostered, it might be a good idea to weed out cards that harp on aspects of 'family history' which that child does not have access to).

And that's it, except for the fun part, which is that if you throw a six you get a Wild Card, which commits you to performing a silly task at the table – 'With your mouth lift a spoon or fork off the table and pass it by mouth to the person on your right' or 'try touching your nose with your tongue while you hum "Happy Birthday".'

I have to be frank – the first time I played this with my children ended in total war because they disagreed about whose turn it was next. But the next time we played it was much more fun and there were no squabbles. The young lady from Slovakia who was staying with us at the time loved it because for once she could follow what was being said. The youngest child in particular adored it, because it gave her an undisputed right to an equal hearing, and she did not have to scream her head off to get it. I can see it being particularly fun for a single-child family for the same reason – everyone has their say on an equal footing. 'Only' children sometimes feel their lives consist entirely of interrupting adult conversations.

Games like this create a party atmosphere which can magically dispel sibling rivalries. But you don't necessarily need a set of special cards to create the same atmosphere. Try the 'two things about my day' game, particularly good when there are people round the table who never get a word in edgeways. Each person talks about two things that happened to them that day – good or bad, happy, sad, funny, infuriating. The person then chooses who goes next, the second person chooses the third and so on.

What has this to do with Christianity, you may ask? Everything. To be serious about letting this faith work its magic in your life as a family, you need to allow your family to be a bit more upfront in talking about – that's *talking about,* not *quarrelling about,* important things in general. An opened-up family that has a habit of talking together will feel more at ease in talking about difficult, way-out things like eternity, death and redemption.

Parlour games of any kind at the table not only discourage squabbles (rather in the manner that good ground-cover plants discourage weeds in the garden) but also put children on an equal footing with adults. But it is also important to put adults on an equal footing with children.

When eating with your own children, don't be a martyr – make the meal one you would enjoy as well. If that means getting the children to do some serving at the table instead of letting you bustle around them like an unpaid waiter then so be it. If that means wine (for adults!), candles and flowers, then make with the corkscrew, candlesticks and vase. If that means putting foods the children 'won't eat' on the table now and again, so be it. The fussy eater might have to fill up with a few doorsteps of wholemeal bread just this once.

Fussy eaters

If that fussy eater is turning your table into a battle ground every day, stop fighting! Young children do not deliberately starve themselves; if you expose them to a balanced diet they will get what they need, or so the theory runs.

And it is a good theory, but you do have to acknowledge that you are largely responsible for what foods they are exposed to. If a child is offered sweets or sugary drinks throughout the day, the edge will have been taken off his or her appetite and the green beans will be left on the side of the plate once again. If you worry that your child will only consume crisps and Tango, you have to ask yourself how the child is getting access to these items.

We are expecting children to have very sophisticated palates now at an early age. For good reasons, children have a natural caution about unfamiliar foods – their caution is a vestige of the way in which our pre-historic ancestors protected themselves against poisoning from the wrong sort of berries or fruit. The fantastically varied food industry of our time, which makes it so easy for parents to offer their children Chinese on Monday, Thai on Tuesday, Italian pizza on Wednesday, American hot dogs on Thursday and fish and chips on Friday, is completely out of tune with children's natural preference for a limited range of trusted foods.

So be patient with the fussy eater. Did you know that it takes, on average, 25 'exposures' to an unfamiliar food before the average child will cautiously try eating it? In other words, if you put a little (always a *little* – large portions also put off fussy eaters) green cabbage on a child's plate once a week it will be nearly six months before you can realistically expect him to put any in his mouth. That is a lot of cabbage.

As for the supposed disappearance of the family mealtime – well, I have my doubts. We are intensely food-obsessed, and the furniture stores still seem to do a roaring trade in tablecloths, crockery and cutlery, not to mention cooking gadgets. Someone must be using all that stuff. Children's obesity has become a matter for Government concern, and everyone agrees that constant snacking, without the proper discipline of mealtimes, is a major factor in obesity. So press on with the family dinner time … and if you find a place at the table for a little spirituality, then blessings be on your cooking.

'... with a glass of wine and your favourite toddler ...'

7

When the disciples sat in the 'upper room' at the first Pentecost, and felt the power of the Holy Spirit enter them, they had a direct personal experience of God with no middle-man involved, no mediation by a priest, leader or parent. When it comes to our children's religious

The Magic of Reading

experience, we can only act as mediators for some of the time. We should do all we can to direct, encourage, help, suggest and prod — but the ultimate aim is for a one-to-one exchange between God and the child. And that is a private conversation in which the child's parents cannot play a part.

Do you have a small baby? Isn't the baby still essentially an extension of yourself, sharing your space and needing you totally? If so, it may be uncomfortable to think of this little, dependent person sharing an exclusive, private conversation with anyone else, let alone with God. If you feel uncomfortable about this then perhaps you need to re-assess your whole view of spirituality and your view of your child as a separate person. You still have not come to terms with your baby's 'otherness'.

I can see an analogy between children's spiritual growth and their relationship with children's books. When you read a story with a small child it is a shared experience. There are three of you in the game of telling a story: the author, the parent and the child. When your older child picks up a book and reads it, the game becomes a two-person affair – you, the parent, are cut out of the two-way conversation between the child and the author.

The child is free to stop, re-start and skip parts of the conversation as he desires. (This is not the case with television, which, even if interactive, drags the child along at the pace and in the time dictated by the programme maker.) Books give your child power over the time he/she is spending time: but also allow a strange adult to make overtures directly to your child. This is why parents feel so strongly about what their children are reading.

The biggest thing in children's literature in recent years has been the remarkable Harry Potter series by J. K. Rowling. From being a penniless (but well-educated) young single mother, nursing cups of coffee for hours in an Edinburgh café while writing furiously in order to get as many words down on paper as she could before the baby woke up, Joanne Rowling has become one of the richest women ever to make money out of writing books, and, thanks to her tenacious grip on the feature films made of her books, is even cited as one of the most influential people in Hollywood.

Success carries criticism with it, and for J. K. Rowling, one particularly vociferous source of criticism has been the Christian fundamentalist movement in the United States. By the time the fourth book in her seven-volume Harry Potter series was published, writer after writer and speaker after speaker had stood up to condemn her books for promoting witchcraft, even Satanism. The books were, it was alleged, bound to be responsible for a massive upsurge in children seeking more information about the occult; and moreover were supporting the growing popularity of Wicca, the official name of the 'religion' of witchcraft.

Some Christian critics homed in on the injunctions in the books of Deuteronomy and Isaiah against practising witchcraft and magic, and argued that on that ground alone, Rowling's books were strictly out of bounds for Christian children. On the outer fringes of the anti-Potter movement are some oddball characters who claim that Rowling is controlled by Wiccans who are using her to subvert the world's children, and those who claim to have found secret symbols and occult messages hidden in the text.

When the Warner Brothers feature film of *Harry Potter and the Philosopher's Stone,* the first book of the series, came out in 2001 a few doughty Christian parents stood outside cinemas holding placards entreating families to boycott the movie. The same thing happened in a small way in Britain, with parents in one Somerset town calling for the film to be banned. Some of these parents just did not like seeing witches and wizards made glamorous; others believed it seriously promoted witchcraft, even un-wittingly; other still perhaps fell into the group who believe that J. K. Rowling has a Wiccan agenda.

Rowling herself flatly and fiercely denies this accusation and anyone who knows anything about her knows that it is sheer nonsense to connect her with occultists of any kind. A protest from one group of parents in one town hardly makes a mass revolt: most parents either do not care about the issue or recognise that far from being under the spell of real-life witches, Rowling is a highly well-read English graduate with a good knowledge of classical and other European mythologies; it is very important to any understanding of the way the book appeals to children to be aware that her interest in magic is a purely literary one.

She made up the spells in her books using her vast and squirrel-like knowledge of magical literature as a support; consequently she is flabbergasted when members of the public approach her at book-signings and whisper furtively that they have 'done all the spells'.

The objectors to Harry Potter point out that the books inspire children to search for witchcraft on the internet and so become drawn into paganism and Wicca. This is a sensible enough prediction – I can well believe that some children may have done this. If the books were the first children's books ever to deal with witchcraft in a light-hearted way, then it would be fair to accuse Harry Potter of starting a trend.

But since children's bookshelves have been groaning with magic, ancient and modern (much of it produced by upright Victorian Christian authors) for as long as children's literature has existed as a separate genre – and magic, moreover, has featured as part of mythology and literature for even longer than that – it seems invidious to single out Harry Potter for criticism.

For this is the main problem for all objectors to Harry Potter: witchcraft and magic are as universal in children's literature as the words 'Once upon a time ...' Magic is so prevalent in children's literature that it is almost synonymous with it. The very idea of wonderful things happening which real-life physics simply do not allow to happen is entrancing to us all, and is embedded deeply in our traditions of writing for children.

In that sentence alone I used two words that are tied up with the idea of magic: for 'wonderful' is just another way of saying 'to be wondered at, to be amazed by' and 'entrancing' can mean much the same as 'enchanting, casting a spell on'. For centuries, whatever we could not explain, we called magic; and when we stopped believing in magic and started believing in science, we went on imagining all the *fabulous* things that magic might be able to do. 'Fabulous', of course, means 'as in a story' – a children's story.

Magic has many roles to play in children's literature; but I believe one which most people are unaware of is as a *template for religious experience*.

For example, it is very common in children's stories for a child to have an unseen friend with whom they alone can converse. It is also very common for ordinary-looking objects to have special powers that are not apparent to the casual onlooker, and for children in stories to find their way to some parallel world which might mirror our own in some way.

A child in a home where spirituality is distrusted, despised or ignored usually leaves the imaginary world of magic behind once she has graduated to more 'grown-up' matters such as make-up, boy bands and dieting (or spots, looking cool and football in the case of boys). But a child who has grown up in a home where spirituality is valued and enjoyed the role of magic in her favourite books is open to possibilities; open to the idea of faith as a power; open to the indescribable satisfaction that rituals can give to those who perform or observe them.

A child who has grown up at ease with the idea of magic in children's books is also able to look at difficult Christian ideas: for example, the meaning of the Eucharist; the idea of the Holy Spirit working among us, or the idea of there being an unseen spiritual dimension to life, and say, 'Yes, I can get the point of that. That resonates with something I read somewhere when I was little. I know how that feels.'

In this way fictional magic can work as a template for religious experience. I first came across the word 'template' as a child, when my mother was showing me how to make patchwork cushions from cotton scraps cut into hexagons (this was a fairly retro activity even when I was young). To help us to keep all the cotton hexagons the same size, and to make it easier to sew them together, we drew them around cardboard shapes drawn with the aid of a flat plastic hexagon called a template. The plastic hexagon was not a patchwork piece, it was not made of the same stuff as the patchwork pieces, and it could not be sewn like a patchwork piece; therefore it could not do the same job as a patchwork piece. But without it we would have been hard put to it to create the patchwork pieces, and the cushion we were trying to make from them, at all.

In the same way, fictional magic is not in itself religious experience; it cannot stand in for religious experience or perform exactly the same emotional function, but it does give us clues as to how religious experience feels, and may even be an essential part of our religious growth.

One aspect of the Harry Potter controversy hit me when my eldest son began his first term at a very traditional and high-achieving Catholic boys' comprehensive. On the first day of school we went with him and all the other first years in their all-black uniforms and strictly policed regulation haircuts. A casual observer might assume this was a private school, looking at the roll of honour on the wall, the masters and mistresses in flowing black academic gowns, the strong-voiced choir singing Latin Masses at the local church. But this is a state school, and the pupils come from all walks of life – the families who turned up for Mass on the first day of term were not the kind of families you see at a privileged fee-paying school occasion.

Looking round at the congregation as we sang hymns so unbelievably traditional that we had not sung some of them since our own school days, I was awestruck. What did we have in common, the parents of these boys who disappeared from our view, one by one, as their names were called out by a black-gowned teacher and they were sorted into their ability groups? Nothing visible. We were multi-ethnic, from all classes and most income brackets below that of the super-rich. Some parents were single, others came as couples. We were all desperately proud that our sons had won places at this school, but what else did we have in common?

The answer was simple – our faith. You couldn't see it or touch it but it was there, binding us invisibly. 'Good heavens,' I thought irreverently. 'It's Hogwarts!'

Unless you have been on another planet for the last four years you know that Hogwarts is the fabulous boarding school for young witches and wizards which is attended by Harry Potter. Since the English are obsessed with schools, a certain amount of debate has centred on what kind of school Hogwarts most resembles. It has been compared to English public schools, quite erroneously, for the children at Hogwarts pay no fees and are clearly not all from rich families. It has been compared with grammar schools, again erroneously, since Hogwarts is, judging by the comic ineptitude of many of the pupils, a comprehensive. Citing it as proof of the benefits of boarding school also misses the point: Hogwarts is a boarding school but through necessity rather than for snobbish reasons – it is sited in a Scottish castle somewhere in the Highlands.

All these analogies are quite wrong. Hogwarts is a voluntary aided school. Its pupils are bound together not by academic ability or their parents' ability to pay fees, but by their 'faith', the invisible something which in real life is baptism into the Christian faith and which in the fantasy world of Harry Potter is magical ability. J. K. Rowling takes the similarity on further. The school is fiercely proud of its traditions. It has rituals and rules handed down by generations of wizards. It has high expectations of pupils and strict discipline. All these will be quickly recognised by parents as being chief among the reasons why voluntary aided/controlled Church schools are so oversubscribed.

The best-known example of the phenomenon of magic working as a template for religious experience is sitting right on your local bookshop shelves: C. S. Lewis's seven Narnia novels, of which *The Lion, the Witch and the Wardrobe* was the first. Lewis wrote these stories with the explicit intention of exploring the Christian ideas of sin, sacrifice, redemption and forgiveness in terms which children would not only understand but also warm to and enjoy, as millions have.

Just in case you are not familiar with the books, here are the bare bones of their story: a group of children enter a magical parallel world centred round an idealised land called Narnia. Ruling Narnia is its creator, a huge, wise Lion called Aslan who is something of an absentee landlord: he comes and goes unexpectedly, sometimes guiding the heroes' steps in pushing Narnia's history to its apocalyptic conclusion.

In the first book, *The Lion, the Witch and the Wardrobe*, Aslan gives himself up to torture and a cruel death in return for the deliverance of one of the children, who has betrayed the rest to the evil White Witch. But not even the White Witch realises that there is 'a deeper magic' than the one she thinks she knows about; this 'deeper magic' brings Aslan back to eternal life. The parallel with the death and resurrection of Jesus is obvious to all who know of it. Subsequent stories show Aslan guiding human children through various adventures in which other parallels with Christian history and the narrative of faith are discernable until in *The Last Battle* the visible Narnia world ends and the children go to the better, 'real' Narnia beyond this world, revealed to be only shadows of God's reality.

There are many irritating flaws in the Narnia books. Lewis's unease with female sexuality, for example, leads him to exclude one of the children from the 'real Narnia' afterlife simply, as far as one can tell, because in growing up and discovering her own sexuality, she does not want to believe any more that Narnia is true. Narnia's all-white ruralism sits uneasily with today's urbanised, multi-cultural Britain, so much so that the moral superiority which Lewis attributes to the fair-skinned, fair-haired Narnians over the 'swarthy' Calormenes who live to the south of Narnia, and whose dress and religious mannerisms have more than a flavour of pantomime-level Islam, is actually offensive.

But it is unfair to blame Lewis for being so much part of his own culture that he could not see its prejudices quite as clearly as we think we can. His (very slight) bias towards boys is typical of his era – in fact, compared with some of his contemporaries, Lewis gives girls more than their usual share of the action. He has a bias against any kind of democracy and towards a more romantic idea of benevolent kingship, but this is completely forgivable in the fantastical context in which he was writing.

Lewis's overt racism is less forgivable: but what is hard to forgive in an Oxford don with rather limited knowledge of the world at large, however, is even harder to forgive in his contemporaries, the critics and Lewis's own publishers, who seemed not in the least concerned that the books might be read by any children who were not 'fair-skinned'.

For all their flaws, the Narnia books remain the most effective, best-loved Christian allegory of all time. They have helped many families to express their faith and perhaps wakened faith in many more. The idea of the 'deep magic' resonates with Christians and with people of other monotheist faiths.

But to many non-Christians, especially those unfamiliar with the Christian story or those who have had a secular upbringing, it comes as something of a nasty shock to discover the author's Christian agenda. 'Such good stories – what a shame it's religious propaganda,' commented one intellectual friend of mine from a liberal secular family. The contemporary children's author Philip Pullman goes further: he has repeatedly condemned the books as 'atrocious', as 'celebrating death' and as 'a massive deception'. Like a child who discovers that the stage magician is using sleight-of-hand, rather than genuine magic, Pullman feels cheat-ed: cheated into feeling sympathy and admiration for a belief-system he despises. Pullman describes the books as 'propaganda in the service of a life-hating ideology'.* His view seems to be mainly based on his own interpretation of the final scenes of the series portrayed in *The Last Battle*, when Narnia comes to an end and the children and their Narnian friends go off to the 'real' Narnia of the afterlife. The idea that a better world exists after this one is unacceptable to Pullman and he believes sincerely that teaching it to children is wicked.

Pullman has seriously misunderstood the final message of the story. A closer look at the Christian view of the relationship between life on earth and life after death would have revealed that far from being a soothing promise of pie in the sky when you die, it is instead an urgent wake-up call; time and again in the New Testament we are exhorted to be ever watchful, live

---

* Pullman has expressed this view many times – this particular quotation comes from an article he wrote in the *Guardian* (1 October 1998). He accused the Narnia series of 'celebrating death' in an article in the *Sunday Telegraph* (January 2002). In reply to a question at a literary festival in 2002, he said of Lewis's Narnia books: 'I realised that what he was up to was propaganda in the cause of the religion he believed in.'

each day as our last: if nothing else remains of Christian beliefs, it should at least be that the here and now matter very, very much. True, the manner in which one girl is forbidden entry to the afterlife because she is showing interest in 'nylons and lipstick and invitations' is not attractive in its rejection of sexuality: but Lewis was, at the time of writing the Narnia stories, yet to get properly to grips with his own sexuality in any case.

Unlike Philip Pullman, most children who read these books adore them and many enjoy spotting the parallels with the Christian story. 'Oh, it's just like Jesus on the cross,' my eldest child, then aged seven, remarked in a slightly blasé tone when I first read *The Lion, the Witch and the Wardrobe* to him. The satisfaction of spotting the allusions to Christ's suffering was considerable. It made me feel sorry for those children who read the stories and do not know to what they allude – they are missing out on the pleasure of recognition. And if the hard-line atheists had their way, schools would be prevented from handing on the traditions and language of religion which give children a handle on what these stories are ultimately about.

Which Books to Choose?

It is mostly in children's books that children first become aware of the existence of religious feeling and first sense the stirring of religious feeling and spirituality within themselves. Because of the independent nature of the act of reading, children's literature is a more fertile field for the awakening of these feelings than almost anything else you can name – trips to church, treks up mountains or school RE lessons all have their part to play, but none has quite the secrecy and independence of reading under the bedcovers.

During my years as a children's books reviewer I would often be asked for a list of 'suitable books' for children. Such a list can never be satisfactory. For one thing, it would be incomplete even if the most assiduous children's librarian or book critic compiled it. For another, certain books might work for one child but leave his best friend absolutely cold.

If you want to become a 'good reading parent' you need to learn the ability to put a range of good books within your child's grasp. Firstly, you need to encourage the reading habit by:

+ **Setting an example.** Do the children ever see you read? This especially applies to fathers, who are least often seen reading by their children.

+ **Making reading into a pleasant family activity** which everyone feels comfortable with. My children jealously guard their 'reading time' between going to bed and lights-out time because it guarantees another half-hour before they have to go to sleep. When your first child is still very young, firmly install the bedtime story into your evening routine – make it something you, the parent, can't help looking forward to: an opportunity to put your feet up in a comfy chair with a glass of wine and your favourite toddler beside you. Bliss.

+ **Keep visiting the local library** and searching for new titles. Read children's book reviews in newspapers – they will tell you about good new books that you can encourage your library to buy in. Persistently ask the staff for books you think they should stock.

+ **Check out second-hand bookshops** – so much cheaper, and as children's books have a shorter reading-life than adult novels, you will find quite recently published stuff.

+ If you are bored with what is on your own shelves and with the local library's stock, **consider a children's book exchange circle** with a group of like-minded friends. Meet up once a month, each bringing a pile of books, and let the children browse and swap (don't forget to write your name inside the front cover of each book if you want to see it again). This works especially well for young children, as picture books work out at a lot of money per minute of enjoyment.

If you really want to know what children's books are like, the only route is to read them yourself. Good newspapers all carry reviews of children's books at fairly regular intervals, and especially around the times of Christmas, Easter and summer holidays. But also expect to do a lot of reading! Titles and covers, especially for books for older children and young adults, can be a poor guide: I have come across many luridly-titled teenage novels with deliberately sexy or provocative titles which turn out to be thoroughly feet-on-the-ground stories in which virtue is triumphant and vice punished.

Anyone who goes within six inches of teenagers has long been wise to the importance of dressing up decent, old-fashioned family values in a 'cool' new outfit. I have on my shelves a book explaining Roman Catholic doctrine for teenagers: on the cover is a photo of His Holiness John Paul II in his youth in the 1950s, wearing a beatnik-style beret and dark glasses. Who are they kidding?

Books that help nurture a child's spiritual growth need not be Christian books by any means. But they should be compatible with Christianity – they should celebrate love, self-sacrifice, selflessness, truth and courage. It might be easier to start with a list of the aspects of children's books that the alert spiritual parent needs to be on guard *against*.

- **Books in which religion, religious services or religious leaders are denigrated;** a great number of authors now think this is a good way of showing their 'cool' credentials. Look out for disparaging remarks about religion or clergy made by key characters.
- **Books in which people who practise a religion are portrayed as inevitably hypocritical, even evil.** You will find repressive Christian parents, sneaky vicars and cruel priests in many books, usually ranged against the natural goodness of the child-hero. This device makes a good story but gives a very skewed view of Christian practice. Philip

Pullman's *His Dark Materials* trilogy is perhaps the most famous example of this type of story, being a long and elaborate attack on the whole concept of an organised religion and the existence of God.

✦ **Books in which the occult is treated with great seriousness** as an alternative religion. Harry Potter is very tame compared with some 'witch' books which are set in far more realistic, less fantastical surroundings than Hogwarts. The idea of witches appeals enormously to teenagers – look at the success of the TV series *Buffy the Vampire Slayer*.

✦ **Books in which children get their way by lying, bullying or any other form of dishonesty and cruelty.** As children's authors are on the whole a pretty responsible crew, there are hardly any such books. One of the most criticised authors of modern times is the late Roald Dahl: when his revenge-filled story books such as *Matilda* and *George's Marvellous Medicine* were first published they shocked adults with the anarchy and violence against adults with which they are filled. But even Roald Dahl filled his books with a basic respect for goodness; his retributive justice against oppressive adults had more resonance for his own generation, brought up in stricter circumstances during the Second World War, than later generations.

A book that makes you feel uncomfortable for any of these reasons need not be banned: banning books only makes them more attractive. But it need not stay in the house for long.

On the positive side, look out for:

✦ **Books that show religious people as normal human beings**. It is rare for a priest or minister to come into a story at all; even more rare for him or her to be portrayed sympathetically. Authors such as Josephine Feeney or Jonathan Stroud allow the clergy to appear as normal people.

✦ **Books that mention churchgoing, at least in passing,**

as a normal activity. Though you may search in vain for such books! Christian children, their schools, their routines of worship, their family prayers, are all more or less excluded from modern children's literature. I have read hundreds and hundreds of 'real life' novels for children of eight and upwards and I think I can safely say that in no more than two or three of them was there any mention of the characters in the story going to church on Sunday. And if they did, they certainly did not regard it as a pleasure. This is not necessarily the fault of individual authors, but that of the publishing business which hates anything in a story that might put off the majority of readers.

✦ **Magic stories in which magic is used as a plot device for rewarding virtue** and punishing evil. The Harry Potter series is the most obvious example of this type. British children's books have a strong tradition of 'fun magic' writers such as Joan Aiken and Diana Wynne Jones, who create worlds in which magic creates as many problems as it solves.

✦ **Real–life stories in which children have experiences** outside the modern indoor pursuits of television watching and PlayStations. Michael Morpurgo's stories, for example, often involve a close interaction between a child and an animal. His short but well-formed stories such as *When the Whales Came* and *The Butterfly Lion* always throw light on human experience through the medium of contact with the natural world. The ever-popular Dick King-Smith writes light-hearted and funny stories often drawing on his own experience as a farmer.

✦ **Stories in which children are away from the control of adults**, and have to make their own moral decisions. This includes just about all the best classic stories, from *Swallows and Amazons* onwards. Part of the charm of the Harry Potter series is that the boarding-school scenario eliminates the presence of parents from most of the action: the children are empowered to act on their own, making mistakes and learning from them. Jacqueline Wilson, who is often regarded as the most popular children's writer of our time, derives much of her appeal from her ability to take a serious, life–shattering issue (homelessness, mental illness, bereavement — to name a few) and see it from inside a child's mind without trivialising the issue or ridiculing the child. Authors such as Lesley Howarth (*The Pits, Mister Spaceman*) and Anne Fine (*Flour Babies, The Tulip Touch*) explore the inner life of teenagers in an offbeat mode — parents can learn a lot just from reading their books.

✦ **Stories which open children's minds to a more spiritual world, or a world with more possibilities than the here and now.** Such stories might range from classics such as Lewis Carroll's *Alice in Wonderland* or Kenneth Grahame's *Wind in the Willows* through to modern classics such as Philippa Pearce's *Tom's Midnight Garden* or Sylvia Waugh's *The Mennyms* series, or Sally Prue's extraordinary *Cold Tom*. In particular, look out for books in which the presence of magic serves to open the mind to new possibilities, unseen worlds and unseen powers. The *Wind on Fire* trilogy by William Nicholson is a very good example: set in an alternative reality, it is an epic in which three children save their tribe from destruction in an exciting and deeply symbolic quest. Look out also for books by Garth Nix, Ursula LeGuin, Sophie Masson and Graham Taylor.

The finest children's literature is always aware of a bigger picture, always pointing away, outside itself. To be aware of books that do this you need, quite simply, to read more of them! And if this list looks like a shameless plug for the children's book industry, then that is precisely what it is. So read and enjoy!

'... a family night.'

8

So how can your spiritual life make your family life happier? Does a family with faith have to be a miserable bunch of repressed weirdos or a suspiciously jolly little band of grinning idiots?

Neither, I hope. Certainly these descriptions do not remind me of any of the families I talked with for this book. Active Christians in Britain

Happy Days and Holidays

today are generally kind, well-meaning people who work daily to put their faith into their lives. and find that doing so gives their lives more meaning and purpose.

The trouble is that so much of the effort seems to be negative. Being a Christian should mean saying 'yes' to things but in practice we end up saying 'No': no late night violent or sexually explicit films, no drugs, no sex. Jesus himself could be very blunt in saying 'no' to activities he knew to be contrary to God. He had a tendency to be 'not very nice' when it came to saying 'no'. In fact he was capable of being downright rude.

On the other hand, it is dispiriting to live with negatives all the time. It's better to consider ways of building enjoyable *positives* into your family life. You can allow your children to grow up remembering their Christian upbringing as a long succession of prohibitions, or you can create memories of fun and warmth that are inextricably linked with the faith they are learning to follow. Which would you prefer?

Family Night

A basic tool of family life is simply doing things together. This has been built up by some American Evangelical groups as the 'family night'. It is a concept which immediately fails to recommend itself to your average cynical Brit, owing to its strong association with that awe-inspiring community, the Church of the Latter Day Saints, commonly known as the Mormons.

My own contact with the Mormons is limited to doorstep encounters with amazingly healthy-looking young American men in dark suits, wearing plastic name tags on their lapels declaring them to be 'elders' despite the fact that they do not look quite old enough to shave.

I confess that, in common with the vast majority of Brits I don't tend to invite the 'elders' in for a chat. I normally explain politely that we are not of their denomination and that we are very content to remain with our own church, thank you very much and God bless you, good luck in your work. Then I close the door. They always seem pleasantly surprised to be told that we are Christians, and are so unfailingly polite and charming, and even sometimes so good-looking, that I fear that one day I shall succumb and allow them into my living room. Then I won't know how to get rid of them.

If this is offensive to any Latter Day Saints, I apologise sincerely. While some of their beliefs are definitely not in line with most other Christian groups, I do admire the way the Mormons have raised family life into an art form. The best known of their family traditions is that whereby committed Mormon families designate one night of the week as the night they stay in with their loved ones: this is a strong commitment and cannot be broken for parties, work, swimming lessons or anything.

The idea of a family night can be used by any family, whether Christian or not. It is especially valuable in busy families where teenage children are getting harder and harder to pin down.

What is a family night for? And who is it for? It is a commitment to share each others' company for an evening a week, and to keep this as a firm 'date' that can't be broken, come hell or high water. Come high water, at any rate. Hell might be harder to get round.

Typically, the family sets aside a regular three-hour slot when the family eats together and shares some recreational activity. How do you know if you would benefit from this practice? Well, it depends how much you see of each other. If you never see your teenager from one day's end to the next, you need a family night. If you eat at different times from your hungry pre-schooler, you need a family night. If you and your partner work different shifts, or go out with different social groups frequently, you need a family night. If you cannot think of any activity you share with your children besides eating and sleeping, you definitely need a family night.

As with everything involving your children, it pays to start early. If you establish a family night routine before children reach the teen years, you have a basis of tradition on which to call when they start crying off as teenagers. Your teenage daughter protests that she cannot be there for family night, due to a crucial nail-grooming session scheduled at her best friend's house? If the family night tradition has been there since she was little, she *may* feel less resentful about keeping to it.

On the other hand, establishing a family night needs careful thought because it is sad to start something that fades away after a few weeks. Think about when the best time would be to set aside three hours or so in the evening and try to discuss it with the rest of the family. What other commitments do the family have? Which member of the family will be least easy to accommodate, or most reluctant to take part?

Consider whether you can manage to keep up the family night as a weekly event. Personally I would hate to commit the same evening a week to a family get together for the rest of my life. There is just too much else to fit into our lives. Sure, we fit everything else around our church commitments, but I doubt we could add a permanent evening commitment on top of that without it falling apart after a few months.

Advice on family nights usually stipulates that you should not accept invitations out for that evening but I cannot see this working out for a busy modern family. For example, I like our family night to be on Fridays; but if some old and dear friends schedule their Silver Wedding anniversary party for a Friday evening, my husband and I are certainly not going to miss it for the sake of the family night which takes place every week.

So unless you can manage a weekly event, a monthly family night would be a good and workable target to aim for. Designate, say, the first Thursday in each month for your special evening. Gather ideas from the rest of the family for what they would like to do on that special evening – they will soon be looking forward to it.

The family night needs an element of democracy to work, which means that you, the parent, may have to make a few bargains to get the children to co-operate. Trade-offs might include a promise that one child's passion for Indian takeaways will be indulged regularly provided the same child foregoes the Playstation 2 for the duration of family night. Or you might have to promise that on no account will you require anyone to play Scrabble, if they really, *really* don't want to.

Once you have fixed on a particular night of the week or month as 'family night', protect it. It's a matter of priorities: that special friends' wedding anniversary party won't happen again, but your daughter's friends' nail-painting session is easily moved or repeated.

Put the answerphone on and switch off your mobiles. Keep the television switched off. While your family night might take the form of watching a video once in a while, this should not be the norm. Family members could take it in turn to 'order' the menu for family night. They could also take it in turn to prepare the meal and clear up afterwards. Or you could take it in turns to be the King or Queen of the day, choosing the meal, the activity, and being waited on by the others.

While the meal part of family night is very important, the activity should be of equal importance. Younger children usually love thinking about food, but older ones, in particular teenage girls, can find the whole business of meals and food oppressive. The family night should be a supportive experience: it is an opportunity for you to show that there is more to family life than eating.

I have to admit that there are long phases in my family's development when I feel we need not a family night, but a non-family night, and plenty of them. Any meal shared by the six of us seems bound to end in tears, loathing, recriminations, screaming, violence and despair. And that's even before we get onto the subject of my cooking.

On the other hand, when we do other things together, simple things like walking in one of the very beautiful parks that are a short drive from our house, we don't quarrel half so much, and even end up feeling cheerful. It may simply be that even though it is part of our routine, eating together is not our strongest bonding activity: a hard fact to swallow, but there it is. For families like us, a family night needs to be centred round something other than food.

Keep changing the activity – and while occasionally it is fun to go out and spend money, try to keep to indoor activities that are easy to organise at short notice. Here are a few ideas, culled from various sources and including some of my own:

+ **Make up a new game** – a snakes and ladders style board game, perhaps, based on the ups and downs of your family's day.
+ **Go on a scavenger or treasure hunt.**
+ **Walk around your neighbourhood with bin bags,** wearing rubber gloves, and collect a bag of rubbish each.
+ **Make a home video** all about yourselves.

+ **Take a present** – a cake, some flowers – round to an old person living alone in your neighbourhood.
+ **Invite a special guest for dinner:** someone you all admire, such as a favourite teacher, or someone lonely.
+ **Tackle a craft project** together.
+ **Clear out your wardrobes and cupboards** and fill some bin bags with charity donations.
+ **Wash and vacuum the car.**
+ **Play charades, games involving acting and dumb-show.** 'In the manner of the word' is a favourite if the players are a widely scattered age group. It works like this: one person, the target individual, goes out of the room and thinks up an adverb – 'gracefully', 'proudly', 'forcefully' etc. The rest of the group, meanwhile, agree on an activity which the target individual will have to act out: climbing Mount Everest, doing the washing up, signing the Magna Carta or whatever can be agreed on. Then the target individual is called back into the room, and has to mime the activity 'in the manner of the word' which he or she has fixed on. The rest of the group has to guess the word. The classic charade of acting out book, film or television programme titles works wonderfully for groups of roughly similar age who share terms of reference.
+ **Stick photos in albums** or get out old albums and look through them.
+ **Make up a puppet show.**
+ **Make a home video of yourselves** pretending you are in an episode of *Star Trek* (or some equivalent popular family television show).
+ **Ring up relatives who live far away** and from whom you have not heard for a long while.
+ **Play a tried and trusted board game** together.
+ **Get one member of the family with a skill to teach the rest of the family** – it could be sewing buttons on, crewel embroidery, tiddlywinks or drawing.
+ **Discuss and plan activities or treats** for each other's

birthdays in the upcoming year: discuss what everyone wants for their birthday.

✦ **Have a fire drill,** or get a first aid book and discuss what to do in emergencies.

✦ **Read a play**, or a few scenes from one, together.

✦ In the summer, **go out** for a picnic or a hike.

None of these are specifically religious activities but they all support the idea of the family as a key unit in society. Faith families might include prayers and readings from the Bible followed by a discussion as a regular feature, followed by a meal and a fun activity.

Inventing Traditions

The force of tradition is very important as a glue for your family. Traditions help a family to stick together because they help to create a family's personal identity. They are part of what defines your family and makes it different from any one else's.

You probably already have some traditions in your family and don't even realise it. Is there a special ritual surrounding the birthday of a family member? Do you have a special game you always play at the grandparents' house, or a rhyme you all shout out at certain critical moments? Our most common family traditions are usually hitched to birthdays. We have birthday cakes, candles and the singing of 'Happy Birthday'. It is not too difficult, nor does it require much imagination, to add some extras to the standard procedure to make a special tradition for your own family. The birthday cake might be a special recipe that is not used at any other time; or baked in a particular cake tin that you keep for that purpose.

Very large families sometimes have different family traditions for the birthdays of individual family members. For example, my elder daughter's birthday falls on 2 January, probably the gloomiest day of the year. Fortunately it is always a day when the theatres and pantomimes are back in action after their Christmas and New Year breaks, so for several years we 'always' went to the pantomime on her birthday. As she got older, it turned to theatre and when the *Lord of the Rings* film trilogy came out, suddenly that birthday became The Day we went to see the new film. For three years!

The Silver Screen

If modern life needed a defining symbol it would have to be a small square screen. Screens of one kind or another – television, films, computer games, the internet – take so much of our attention and are so fascinating that they play a significant role in cutting the family members off from each other.

'I think most of my battles with the outside world, as a Christian parent, are to do with what's on television,' says Andrea, an unorthodox Christian whose four children go to three different churches every Sunday. 'The list of things I feel happy about them watching gets shorter and shorter.'

A lot of Christian parenting, it sometimes seems, takes the form of switching off the television. This feels extremely negative. We hate saying 'No' all the time. But Teresa Crabtree, who has eleven children, does not see her battle with the television as negative but as a kind of rebellion against the world. She knows that her teenage children like the idea of rebellion; she is particularly adept at getting them to rebel against the conformist society which dictates which television programmes they should or should not consider cool. She says:

> They are discovering that to be a rebel you don't have to be involved in some kind of political rebellion. As Christians we have the chance to be rebels all the time, in our lives – when you have to turn off the television you are rebelling against something on the grounds it goes against God's will. We turn against it and say, 'Jesus doesn't want us to watch things like that!'

> I think children quite like being rebels. They quite like boasting to their friends, 'I'm not going to do that — it's against my religion!' They like the feeling of going against the tide.

Her feeling is shared by many Christian families I have spoken with. They tend to regard the television as an enemy, not as a babysitter. Maybe this is a middle-class attitude, but I don't think so.

At the most basic level, television is hated for the amount of time it takes up, time your child could be spending running about getting tired, building dens, playing interactive make-believe games, doing homework or tidying his or her room. But most of all it is resented for the values it imports into the living room.

Do you need proof that children are influenced by what they see on television? One mother says:

> I know that after watching *The Simpsons*, my nine-year-old son would start talking in this awful cocky way, wise-cracking like Bart Simpson. So I started timing dinner to coincide with the programme's regular slot and that meant we had to give it up for a while. My son stopped the cocky talking very fast.

No one ever went to their grave saying, 'I wish I had watched more television', and common sense dictates that if you can cut back the amount of television your children watch, you will cut down the influence it has on their lives. In addition you can emphasise the positive, as the old song says. Scour the television schedules for things you would really like them to watch, and make sure their television diet includes:

✦ **History programmes** — very fashionable nowadays and done with tremendous pizzazz. Even with the elaborate visualisation techniques now normally used, it is a bit of an effort for children to listen to one historian talking about a single subject for half an hour to an hour. It's an effort well worth encouraging them to make.

✦ **Nature and science programmes** – the acceptable face of sex and violence and a way to start talking about the wonderful world God has made.

✦ **Quiz programmes** – so what's wrong with *Who Wants to Be a Millionaire*? The format may be tacky and the questions feeble, but at least it makes a virtue of knowledge, as opposed to ignorance.

✦ **Dramas** adapted from classic literature.

✦ **Any broadcast introducing a different art form** – whether painting, opera, pottery – which opens out into the world beyond television.

You can do your child nothing but good if you totally eliminate:

✦ **Early morning television aimed at pacifying small children.** Children are at their most alert and imaginative when they wake up in the morning. Their alertness and creativity are gifts. Sitting them in front of early morning television is a great way of throwing these gifts away. We know this from our own experience. Of course for over-worked, tired parents, those quiet morning hours in bed together may be among the most precious of the week, so if you cannot bear to give up that little luxury, at least do not make it a daily habit.

✦ **Violent programmes and explicit sex shown after 9.00 p.m**. In Britain the television companies have agreed not to show material unsuitable for children before this time. But parents need to aware that the 'nine o'clock watershed' has been described, for example, by distinguished broadcasters such as Jon Snow, as being too often treated as an obstacle to be overcome, rather than as a benchmark to be observed. Schedulers, who are more concerned to win viewers among the 18–35 age group than among the under-twelves, are rather more likely to ask themselves, 'Can we slip this in before 9.00 p.m.?' than 'How can we make what is shown before 9.00 p.m. more enriching for children?'

✦ **Soaps.** Much is made of the 'gritty' storylines of the soaps, but for 'gritty' read 'over the top, unrealistic and completely daft'. My chief problem with soaps, as far as their effect on children is concerned, is in the way characters talk to each other. The accepted wisdom among soap writers is to cram as much discord into their storylines as possible along with bullying, cheating, swearing, lying and general yelling. There are very few examples of soaps in which characters seem able to talk to each other reasonably or politely — script writers, probably rightly, feel such dialogue would be too dull for the viewer. Children pick up the form of discourse they are exposed to very quickly.

Above all, share their television watching with them. Don't let them watch in solitude. I find it hard to sit doing nothing while watching television — there are just too many other things to do — but I can usually find some task that I can bring into the room during the children's television time, whether sorting socks or paying bills. As a child I hated my parents making clever comments about my favourite programme while I was watching it, but I did not mind them making gentle remarks about it later on.

If you do not want your children watching television in the same room as you for whatever reason, find somewhere in the house for the television which is not the child's bedroom. Anywhere else — the landing, the closet, the kitchen, the hall, the garden shed. Just not the child's bedroom. Now I am very aware that this sounds an impossible expectation, and I am also aware that millions of lovely, balanced families have televisions in their children's rooms and no one suffers any visible effect. But I am also aware that the parents cannot possibly know what their children are watching.

I have talked to many families with no television in their homes and I have the distinct impression that this is more common in faith families than in non-faith families. For example, the ultra-orthodox Hasidic Jews among whom we lived for seven years in north-east London generally do not have televisions in their homes. One memorably described the television as 'an open sewer running through your living room', which seems a harsh way of describing *Ground Force*. Whatever the children of those huge, orderly Stamford Hill families may be deprived of, they certainly never showed signs of suffering television withdrawal.

Working in my study one sunny day, I was entertained by singing coming from the garden of one of our Hasidic neighbours. Peering out, I saw a deeply nostalgic sight which took me back to my own childhood, when television meant an hour of children's programmes at teatime and no more: a little girl, aged about nine, with pigtails and spectacles, was dancing and singing on her own in her back yard.

For about two hours this delightful child acted out an entire musical production by herself – maybe something she had been taken to, or seen at school. She was lost in a world of pure imagination, summoned from within herself. If she had had a television in the house, would she have been doing this? It is impossible to say for sure, but I fear the truth is that she would not.

Edward Hadas, an American-born financial analyst who, since becoming a Christian several years ago, now gives lectures on ways parents can tap into the strength of faith for their children's sake, lays great stress on 'vigilance' as a parent – the need for us not only to be aware of what our children are doing but to be looking out for the 'teachable' moments in their lives. He feels that a major obstacle for vigilance is that 'great family peace-maker', the television. 'When you read how many murders, how many sex acts are broadcast every year it is clear that no parent can be confident that he knows what his child is watching,' he says.

He gave up having a television in the house when his three children were small and says that the most remarkable thing about the experience was that:

> ... there was no downside. No disadvantage at all. I guess they were never quite so *au courant* with popular things as some of their friends – but from the parent's point of view, if you have no television in the house at all, you have one less thing to argue about. That's a blessing for a start.
>
> You don't have to make all these complicated decisions about whether this or that show is acceptable. You are spared all that, you can just read aloud to them and go out to the movies together.
>
> There are so many advantages to doing without television and so many disadvantages to having the thing, I just don't see why more parents don't do without it ...

he concludes with a cherubic smile (while his interviewer – me – squirms at the thought of living without her treasured collection of Sean Bean videos).

Edward has a good point. Having no television gives you a certain feeling of licence that other parents do not share. Some no-television families have reported to me that their children are envied by their friends for their impressive knowledge of the movies – their parents make an effort to take them to 'everything' as a kind of compensation for not having television. I know another no-television family who always holiday in hotels with gigantic multi-channel televisions in their rooms and happily let the children bask in the cathode rays as much as they like – while they are on holiday.

If you are not going to ban the television altogether you still need to 'accentuate the positive, eliminate the negative', as the song says. This means that if you have to prohibit a film or television show that you are not happy with, always soften the blow with a suggested alternative. Being a vigilant parent as far as television is concerned can mean paying rather more attention to the television magazines than otherwise, digging out the little-advertised but worthy programmes which you can tempt the children with as a compensation from being banned from watching *EastEnders*. The same principle applies to computer games: if you ban the latest must-have shoot-em-up game, you need to be the first on the block with the latest less-violent alternative, a Harry Potter game or its equivalent.

Faith on Holiday

One great way to accentuate the positive for many families is to go on some kind of organised holiday or retreat which brings them together with other families of their own faith in a specifi- cally faith-based context. My family and I have tasted a typical holiday of this type, run by Catholic People's Weeks, an educa- tional charity which organises fairly low-cost family weeks and long weekends throughout the year.

The first time we went on one of these week-long sessions was terrifying, at least in prospect. I made the booking almost without telling the rest of the family what I was doing as I was sure that if I consulted them too much they would shy from the whole idea like frightened deer.

My husband, who has a comprehensive and passionate knowledge of early church music, dreaded the idea of spending so much time with (a) complete strangers and (b) folk music on badly-strummed guitars. My children were aghast at the idea of having to 'make friends' with strange children who, they were certain, would all know each other well beforehand.

Well, there were some guitars, but we all found we didn't mind them a bit as they were pretty competently strummed. And yes, there were children there who all seemed to know each other already, but at least three out of my four children found someone to talk to, which is a good average for us. And what my husband and I had not taken account of in our fears was the intense relief we would feel at sitting out under a spring night sky with bottles of wine quietly being circulated and discussing God, Jesus, the Holy Ghost, the Afterlife and other aspects of our faith with people who did not think we were mad, but indeed actually shared our beliefs. And – now this was the best bit – they were charming, bright people, too!

The weeks are informal but well organised so as to mix pleasure and devotion. There is morning prayer each day and either a Mass or a Eucharistic service, devised by the adults, teenagers and children working in groups. The mornings are taken up either with discussions and liturgy workshops or with something more directly informative – a talk on Old Testament prophecy, church stained glass, aid to the Third World or something else relevant to the week's theme.

The afternoons are free and often a short evening formal session follows lunch and precedes a bit of fun. I have seen an impromptu concert with children and adults doing their 'party pieces'; an all-generations quiz; a 'hot seat' session in which teenagers interrogated adults about their faith. By this time, as a rule, a makeshift bar is open for (brisk) business serving beer, wine and soft drinks and the whole affair takes on the air of a very large family gathering.

Older parents whose children can be left at home for a couple of days have a huge variety of spiritual holidays to choose from: every type of church organises retreats of one type or another or can recommend organisers. The adult-only retreat is the most common. 'It was wonderful,' said one over-stretched mother returning from the first adults-only retreat she had been on for years. 'We studied the writings of Julian of Norwich; it was very academic, which I liked, I sat and made notes, and felt like a student again.'

There are a wide range of organisations running similar experiences for children and teenagers, such as Crusaders, the outward-bound style holiday organisation which has run Christian holidays with the slogan 'effective Christian living' for 100 years (and which specialises in activity camps for children and teenagers), or MasterSun, which runs Bible study holidays as well as more traditional seaside and ski resort breaks.

Some faith-based schools run their own pilgrimages – many Catholic schools, for example, encourage young people to accompany disabled people to Lourdes in the south of France. The experience can be intensely moving, maturing and enormous fun. Being able to look back on experiences like this help your child to grow up with positive memories of being in a faith family, not negative ones.

Above all the retreat/faith holiday experience refreshes your faith. Depending on the style of retreat you choose – monastic or sociable, academic or laid-back – you are thrown together with other people who share your faith, and who have ex-perienced the same kind of setbacks to faith that you have experienced. Coming home from a holiday like this is like emerging from a particularly inspiring sales convention, or from the most uplifting church service imaginable – you feel you can do anything, cope with anything life throws at you – and above all you feel you are not alone.

'... a family service ...'

9

We were in York for the weekend. My husband had long nursed an ambition to attend a really top-quality choral service at the Minster. You know the kind of thing – full organ, sun filtering through ancient stained glass windows, choir in ruffs – the lot. So naturally he had been looking forward to our York weekend for months.

Please Don't Bring Your Laser Gun to Church

We had our one-year-old child with us, our pride and joy, so we found a seat near the aisle and parked the buggy, festooned with interesting little toys on strings, bottles of milk and the usual drapery of blankets and muslin squares, in exactly the right spot for our precious lamb to have a good view of the choristers.

All was fine as we took our seats and the baby gurgled and smiled. Just before the choir and clergy walked in, a perfect silence of expectation fell. For some subconscious, instinctive reason I glanced around behind me for the first time since finding our places. It was then I realised that not only was our son the only person in the church under five; he was the only person under thirty, and I suspect my husband and I were the next youngest.

Just then the baby made a little noise, a tiny, friendly 'glah, glah' noise, just testing the echo, as it were. As noises go, it was hardly noticeable. But in that vast cavern of rustling silence, where heads would turn if a pair of reading glasses were dropped to the floor, it might have been a police siren.

'This isn't going to work,' I whispered to my husband. 'Don't ask me why. It just isn't.' And I scarpered, pushing the buggy out of the church just as the choir and clergy entered. To his eternal credit, my husband followed me, sad but trusting. We both knew the cut-glass silence of that place was no environment for a happy little baby boy, and that to stay would have been to endure an hour of embarrassment.

If you want to get a really energetic discussion going among a group of Christian parents, what topic would you suggest? World poverty? The break-down of the family? The liturgy?

No, if you want to get a roomful of Christian parents really worked up, ask them, 'Have any of you had problems taking your children into church?' and the room will explode with opinions and horror stories.

When my children were small I would come out of church feeling I had done an hour's sparring with Frank Bruno – but without the bonhomie – rather than an hour of worship and contemplation of the infinite. I am not alone. Angela, mother of three girls, sighed:

> My worst moment in church? When my daughter dropped a box of marbles during the two-minute silence on Remembrance Sunday and every single marble hit the ground like a bullet before rolling, slowly and noisily, the entire length of the marble-floored church. Why did we have a box of marbles with us? That's another story.

Another young mother told me:

> We took our three-year-old to a Saturday evening Mass in a Catholic church in New York. Afterwards the priest told us that he didn't want the 'kid' in his church again. He said it would be better if one of us stayed at home with our child.

A father of three asked:

> What do I do when my three-year-old stands in the middle of the aisle and lifts up her dress to show everyone her new knickers? I have this awful feeling that the priest thinks I've put her up to it. I just want to disappear down a hole.

Only a tiny minority of people in this country go to church nowadays; but those who do fall into two main groups. Unfortunately these two groups have very little in common. One group is principally composed of the older generation of churchgoers, aged fifty and upwards. As a rule, they don't have small children living in their homes, and if they once did, the memories of parenthood are fading into a rosy haze.

On the other side are the young parents of small children, people whose faith has often been reawakened by the birth of those small children. Many of the people in this group have not been to church before, or not since their own childhood.

The young parents arrive loaded as if planning an overnight stay. The buggy is festooned with bottles for plugging sudden unwelcome howls, toys that have been allowed in as part of a complicated bargaining process ('OK, you can bring your laser gun as long as you don't shout "boring church, boring vicar" again'), a small library of picture books and a battery of crayons and chocolate biscuits which will leave their mark on every item of clothing within five yards.

Well before the minister has walked in, the fun starts. The crayons are beginning to roll in a steady tinkling waterfall across the uneven medieval seats of the oak pews – funny how you never noticed before that the seats slope forwards – and onto the stone floor, and the children scuttle under the pews noisily to retrieve them from under the feet of ominously unsmiling over-fifties.

One of the children nearly always bangs its head on re-surfacing, and sets up a fabulous howling. The grey heads are starting to turn around and send bad vibes across the church to the mums and dads. Or so the mums and dads imagine.

Once the service has actually begun, things settle down a little – the opening hymn and the spectacle of the minister rolling into the church in outlandish garb are always a good distraction. The children forget their argument over the crayons and instead turn their minds to raiding the chocolate biscuit hoard.

But this brief truce is just that, a brief truce. After another ten minutes, the grey heads' secret, deadly weapon, the church heating system, is being implemented. Because old people feel the cold badly, and because most people who go to church are old, clergy seem think it only kind and reasonable to blast their churches with hot air during services.

But children have warm little bodies, always on the go. They are plump and active, and do not mind a little chill in the air – on the contrary, an overheated room makes them irritable and unhappy. Within a few minutes of the temperature hitting 65°F, at least half the children in the church are fidgety and distressed, and start demanding something to drink (thirst having been increased by the chocolate biscuits). The smaller babies begin to cry, their faces red and unhappy, and only stop crying as soon as Mum has pity and takes them outside. Toddlers like to take the problem into their own hands by taking off their clothes. So the weekly under-fives striptease and screaming match begins, every Sunday morning at a church near you.

By the time the panicked mums have persuaded the children back into their clothes, and, if they are wise, released the babies from a few layers, the bad vibes from the grey heads are wafting through the dust-filled air of the church laced with arsenic, or so the mums and dads think, as they guiltily get out the crayons again and try to persuade the children to sit quietly and do some colouring.

There is always at least one child who has to run up and down the church, as delighted with the excellent run-up as an England fast bowler, and as pleased with the acoustics as a tenor in the Carnegie Hall. This child's parents have a difficult choice. Do they ignore the child and thus court more death-ray stares from the grey heads, or should they give everyone a good laugh by giving chase up the church?

And there is always at least one child who riots uproariously until frogmarched out of the church door by a parent, the child wearing an expression of triumph suggesting that the score so far today is Toddler 1, Mummy 0.

After an hour of desperately trying to keep children in one place and, if not absolutely quiet, then at least in a more or less non-violent state, parents feel bruised, exhausted, dispirited, angry, misunderstood, unappreciated or a combination of any of these. They have barely been able to notice the prayers, readings or sermon, let alone listen to them. They may be aware of having scored some kind of triumph – we 'got through it' for another Sunday. But in their hearts, these parents find it hard not to resent what they see as the disapproval of the rest of the congregation. These are unspeakably unholy thoughts for the weekly act of worship, and a rotten way to start the week.

What is going wrong? The answer is simple: we expect churches not to have children in them. It seems that in the eyes of the world, children and church just don't mix. This is a terrible misconception. Churches should have children in them on Sundays because children are central to Christianity.

We can guess from the Gospels that Jesus himself, as he preached through towns and villages, was always followed by a gaggle of children. Children were underfoot all the time, either at their parent's elbows in the workplace, learning skills for adulthood as Jesus himself did in his father's workshop, or scurrying about the market place, doing – or avoiding – chores.

Teresa, mother of eleven, remarks:

> Calvary wasn't quiet. It would have been bedlam and there would be children there too. When I go to Mass I think of it as a time machine: Jesus is on the cross again, and he is comforted by us being there for him. So I reason that if was possible for those who loved him to be a comfort to him in

that noisy place, then part of me can still be there with him when I am in church with my children.

The quiet chatter of a couple of toddlers, the gurgling of a baby — these are not disruptive or unpleasant sounds. They are lovely sounds and are an essential part of life. Adults make far more noise than children: ever tried to hear yourself talk in a noisy bar? Adults have larger lungs, deeper voices. And there are more of them.

Places without children have an uncomfortable falseness about them, like those hedonistic holiday resorts that are for 'couples only'. The world is not made up of 'couples only' and to pretend so is to inhabit a fantasy that may be deliciously relaxing for the duration of a holiday. For childless couples, it is intensely painful to be reminded of other people's fertility all the time and a child-free holiday must be a welcome respite. But I doubt if most of the people at child-free resorts fall into this category. A place continually without children has no sense of the future, no visual reminder of the purpose of life: such a place lives entirely in the present and the past.

So why do the grey heads turn at the sound of children? The reality is that much of the 'disapproval' which young parents sense is imaginary. Put yourself in the grey heads' place: if you hear a loud noise behind you, do you not instinctively turn your head to see what is making the loud noise? Might you not turn round instinctively, just in case the scuffling, banging sound is old Mrs Biggins falling over again?

Secondly, and very sadly, the sound of a child in church is in some congregations just so unusual that the grey heads, even those in deepest contemplation of the Mystery of the Eucharist, just cannot help themselves. If they stare, it may be out of interest and even delight rather than disapproval.

For all that, though, the disapproval can be very real and very unpleasant. I remember feeling immensely proud of my children during a beautiful sung Latin Mass in a London church. They were being very good, especially the youngest who was only three at the time and more used to the less difficult 'family' service. She spent the service sitting backwards in the pew because in that position she could watch the choir and their conductor in the organ gallery at the back. This fascinating sight kept her fairly happy and she was relatively angelic during the homily. There were a few dropped crayons, but no voices raised above whispers. Her older sister and brothers were mostly too enraptured by the soaring voices of the choir to fidget.

But half way through the Mass I became aware of a steady hissing, a constant muttering noise behind us. At first I had supposed it was some lady saying over her Rosary but suddenly I caught the words, 'and now we'll see if they can behave'. These words were uttered quite audibly and the speaker could certainly not have been following the words of the Mass to be able to say them.

I turned my head and with a chill I saw a woman, not elderly, not poor, not obviously distressed, with her eyes fixed on my children. *My* children. Her lips were moving in a steady stream of invective and vitriol. I caught 'Just can't keep still these days . . . Sort them out for good . . .' and various other phrases that I have blanked from my mind. It was of course the behaviour of someone with an unbalanced mind, though if I were in the least bit superstitious, the words 'evil eye' would have popped into my head. Instead I decided to feel very sorry for this poor woman and ignore her as best I could, which was not easy.

Anyone who becomes so transfixed by the presence of children in church as this poor soul is simply in need of help — that she is there in the church is no reflection on the minister or priest, or the rest of the congregation. As parents we have to accept that such people cannot be turned away from the church. But I took a long time to realise this. Ten years before this episode, I was in York Minster on that fine Sunday morning, chickening out after thirty seconds rather than let my little child stay in the church. It took me over a decade to realise that my children have a right to attend church; *as long as they are not unduly*

disruptive, or spoil a special one-off event such as a wedding, I have a
duty to them and to myself to take them there without fail.

   Churchgoing does not need to be unbearable and no parent
who wants to become part of a faith community should be put
off by a little bit of wriggling in the pew. So here's a survival kit
for families with young children. Start off with this plan from
your child's earliest days and you will find that one day you will
be looking forward to going to church together.

Stress-Free Worship

Start when they are tiny

Even though church seating is rarely adapted to the needs of the
modern baby (ever tried to find a place for a baby's car seat in a
nineteenth century pew?) there is no doubt that the sooner you
start taking your child to church, the easier it gets later on. If you
work hard at making your baby feel part of things, you will be
rewarded. Make sure the child can see what is 'going on'. Even
if this means keeping up a whispered running commentary,
pointing out what the minister is doing, where the lady who is
playing the music is etc, it is well worth it. Turn your running
commentary into a weekly routine; tiny children love repetition,
so make the most of the fact that the service follows the same
pattern each Sunday.

   If you have a special picture book that relates to the service,
point out a particular picture corresponding to each of the different stages of the service and do this each time so that the baby
learns the sequence, associating the actions of the minister with
the pictures in the special book. If there is a sermon, and nowhere
else you can take the baby, have a different book kept aside for
looking at during the sermon. When the congregation sings or
speaks together, do this softly and clearly close to the baby's ear.
Long before he or she can talk, the baby will recognise the words
and tunes, and will get excited to hear them again.

Go to church every week

One reason why Catholic churches are generally fuller than Anglican ones, in the United Kingdom at least, is that the Catholic Church designates every Sunday as a 'holy day of obligation'. The Catholic Church says, in effect, that if you are one of us, you have to go to Mass every Sunday unless you have a darned good excuse, and this applies to adults as well as children. 'Darned good excuses' begin in the region of serious illness and move up the scale towards being stranded in the Gobi Desert.

Thanks to this rigid rule, there is no debate every week about whether or not anyone 'feels like' going to church because the pressure is to go whatever you feel like. Nor is there any question of pretending that a child is 'too young to understand' church, a common excuse put forward *by parents* for not taking their children to church. Catholics do not see it that way: as one Catholic mother put it, 'when you are fourteen, it's good to be aware that God gives you some credit for just turning up', an idea that would cause sharp intakes of breath and raised hands from many Christians who hold more to the view that if you cannot attend church with the right attitude, you had better not attend at all.

We don't expect children to understand the inner meaning of worship, but we do believe that when they are old enough to understand that inner meaning, it helps for them to have a familiar framework in which to place their understanding.

The usual arguments put forward *by children* for not going to church are:

It's boring

It is worship, not entertainment.

I don't feel holy

We don't go to church because we feel holy. We go because we don't feel holy.

I do feel holy and I can worship at home on my own
> Yeah, yeah. Jesus was very clear about worship being a group activity: 'where two or three are gathered in my name . . .' We are part of that group.

I have to meet my friends
> Meet them after Mass.

I don't believe in God
> Well, your parents do and we don't think you are really old enough to be certain if you believe in God or not; for now, as long as you are part of our family, you come to church with us.

We didn't go last week so why do we have to go this week?
> Because we didn't go last week.

Children are creatures of routine, and have short attention spans. A routine which recurs once a month is hard for a small child to get used to. But give a child a routine which recurs every *week* without fail and he will fall into it happily enough. We have always found that if for any reason we missed Mass one week, the children were more restless and rebellious the week after.

As the years go by, the practising Catholic of any age learns to fit life around going to church rather than the other way around. As a convert it took me a long time to get used to this.

Have a 'God Bag' ready

This was a name in our family for a battered old handbag filled with books, paper tissues and spare coins for the collection. It is worth having such a bag ready for taking to church every week. Make sure its contents are relevant. Stick to religious books, children's Bibles and illustrated children's prayer books rather than ordinary secular picture books.

As for toys, when the children are very small, and if you feel very anxious about the grey heads, opt for the least noise-making things you can find, for example a rag doll with a scarf so that a toddler can play at putting it to bed, a hanky that you can tie into different bunny-rabbit shaped knots which the toddler can then undo, pipe-cleaners for bending into funny shapes or fuzzy-felt shapes on a board. Try to keep a limit – one toy per child, for example. Establish an idea of what is appropriate to bring into church. Dolls and action figures are probably more acceptable than laser guns, swords or other blatant symbols of violence. Anything that can be fought with, or which emits piercing electronic noises, is a bad idea; anything cuddly which is silent when dropped is highly acceptable.

Expect some interesting theological arguments: why, after all, should a Barbie doll, which not only glorifies an unattainable female 'ideal' shape but also markets sexuality to children, be 'acceptable' in church, if an old-fashioned sword, a symbol of chivalry and gallantry, is not? (And don't say that the answer is, 'because you can fight with a sword, not with a Barbie doll'. You clearly have never even *tried* fighting with a Barbie doll. Those pointy feet can be vicious.)

Whatever your chosen toys, don't unpack them from the God Bag as soon as you walk into church. The toys are a last resort. The children need to get the message that they are in church to pray and be with God, and to try and do this for as long as they can manage, even if it is only a few minutes. Keep your goodies in the bag and bring them out one by one, putting each back before producing the next. It makes them more interesting (and saves a lot of scrabbling about under the seat at the end of the service, too).

The ideal 'God bag' includes: a few religious-type books, frequently refreshed; crayons (if you can find kindergarten crayons which are triangular in cross-section, grab them, because they don't roll about); blank paper for drawing on; the cherished toy; a small bottle of water; money for the collection; paper tissues, and that should be it. Once children are past the tiny baby stage, it is not really necessary to bring in armfuls of stuff.

Oh, and please, please don't bring food. It only causes problems, and resentment among other children in the church!

Choose a friendly church, and the right service

'We church—tasted for some time before finally settling on our present church,' said Alison, a mother of two. Alison came to her faith on her own, and living in central London, did not have a 'home' church to return to. She settled eventually for a popular, quietly Evangelical church with a thriving Sunday activity programme for children which made the children feel they were part of the service, not a peripheral.

Most churches have a family service of some kind each Sunday, one where small children are welcomed and which is themed to be attractive to children in some way. The only trouble with this arrangement is that some churches make it aggressively clear that they want children to go to *that* service and to no other. Ideally all services should be child-friendly; but the introduction of the special Family Service has led to a kind of ghetto worship mentality. A very British approach to encouraging children into church is to turf them out again as soon as, or even before, the service has begun.

I don't know exactly how many churches still maintain the sinisterly-nicknamed 'crying room', an area set aside behind soundproof doors to which unhappy babies can be dragged. The message which the 'crying room' conveys to parents is: bring your children into church if you must, and be grateful that when, by our dour looks and cold demeanour, we force to remove your distressed child, you are not actually turned out into the rain.

More well-meaning as a solution is the typical church crèche with toys and games of an everyday, secular nature. Fine for under-fives, but once again, the message to parents and their children is: Church is for grown-ups only. Children need not concern themselves with God. Play with these Duplo bricks instead.

More complex to organise, but more satisfying for the children, are services which involve the children themselves. The involvement might be on a practical level: there might be children reading prayers or passages from the Bible; children helping to take the collection up to the altar; children serving at the altar; not to mention children singing or playing instruments. The involvement might be on a liturgical level: the minister might make a point of addressing children in the congregation directly or there could be a parallel children's service taking place in the church hall or side room, which joins up with the 'main' service part of the way through the service.

Some ministers celebrating Eucharistic services gather children round the altar at the most solemn part of the service: I have found this highly effective as the children feel immensely important, but the priest needs nerves of steel, since accidents can happen. The first time I saw this practice, my two-year-old trotted willingly up to the altar, an imposing granite block, and disappeared behind it. A few minutes later there was a howl of 'Ouch!' and a long-drawn-out wailing as our son re-emerged from behind the altar, having tried to dive under it and thumped himself on the head.

Accept that church is different

A father of four told me:

> Church is quite unlike anywhere else that children go. It is not like school, though you may meet friends there and the readings are, of course, 'lessons'. It is not like someone else's house, though you have to be polite. It is not like a museum or gallery, though there may be beautiful or interesting things there.

It is not like a play or concert, though you have to be quiet for much of the time and there is certainly something being enacted up at the altar which to a child may seem very like a drama. Above all, it is not like home: the atmosphere is formal, nobody is supposed to shout or fool about, and parents are not primarily paying attention to the children.'

It is little short of hypocritical to encourage children to believe that churchgoing is 'like' any other experience in their lives. Children accept the idea of its uniqueness much more readily than parents do. Children can see that this is a place where we just *don't* eat sweets and crisps, we just *don't* chatter or run up and down, but we *do* join other families in actions that will live in your child's memory for ever: acts of thanksgiving, of saying sorry, of praise, of singing and of smiling and shaking hands with each other.

Most of all, church is not showbiz. 'But it's boring!' moaned the eleven-year-old daughter of a friend of mine. 'It's *supposed* to be boring,' snapped her mother, earning explosions of laughter and the eternal mockery of her family. Still, my friend had a point: if we go to church expecting to be entertained, then we are regarding it as a form of performance, not as an interactive piece of worship.

Associate churchgoing with a treat

If you want your children to look back with affection on their childhood churchgoing habit, it makes sense to go to a little trouble to sweeten the memories. The church we go to regularly is close to a beautiful urban park, and many parents make the most of this, following up the church service with a session in the adventure playground or hot chocolate and Danish pastries at the café. If this is not possible, at least make sure that the coming home from church is pleasant: clear away the breakfast things before you leave, and have treats in store for when you come home.

It is a great help, too, if your child has friends who attend the same church. Let children and teenagers meet up afterwards; sensible ministers make this easy with church hall coffee sessions, special teen services and so on. Sitting through a 'boring' service is less painful if it means some social interaction later on.

Look ahead to next week

It is so easy to be taken by surprise by church every week. A few minutes of looking into the prayer book or missal to see what will be happening next week can pay great dividends. If you know what the Gospel or other readings are going to be next Sunday, you can prepare your children ahead of time, making it easier for them to follow what is going on.

Don't fret about behaviour

Much anxiety about children's behaviour in church is entirely in the mind of the parent. Teresa Crabtree, a mother of eleven who teaches the Catholic catechism in her parish, puts it like this

> When your children misbehave, bear in mind that your children are probably more bothersome to you than they are to God. God is not that worried if someone is kicking the seat or keeps dropping their book. His patience is infinite. But your children's grotty behaviour can be God's way of teaching you to try to be patient, too.

If you have to discipline children during church, do it lovingly and in as tactile a manner as possible. Don't issue threats such as, 'You'll catch it once I get you home...' Take a wriggly or bickering youngster in your arms and say the prayers close beside their ears, encouraging them to join in. If you are a Catholic, gently take a little one's hands and make the sign of the cross with them. Talk afterwards about bad behaviour; don't take children outside as a punishment unless it is a special occasion such as a wedding, which is being irreparably spoiled.

I try to keep physical contact with my children in church, especially during prayers when I want them to understand that I am praying for and with them. This contact might be just a pat on the shoulder or a hand on the arm now and again — it's just my way of saying 'I'm glad you are here with me'.

What you do, they will do

Even though the children seem totally absorbed in their own little world of fidgeting and complaining, your behaviour before, during and after Sunday worship is setting them an example which eventually they will begin to copy. Even into their teens, their attitude to religion is more a matter of the heart than the head; they will go along with something that feels good.

If you obviously look forward to going to church, they will understand that it is something worth doing; if they can see you are happy being at church, they will learn to be happy too. If they see you are miserable, cross and continually glancing at your watch, they will learn that this whole church business is an utter waste of time. Do the children see you greeting friends among the congregation, or do you sweep in and out looking straight ahead of you? Are you joining in enthusiastically or sitting on the sidelines? There is an American story of a father who put one dollar into the collection and then after the service complained about the singing, the décor and the sermon. 'It's not bad for a buck, Dad,' his small son replied.

If you join in the hymns cheerfully (but not embarrassingly), your children are more likely to follow. It is amazing how few adults actually bother to sing properly in church, yet they wonder why children seem uninvolved.

In our family, we experience what I think of as the Sunday Lunchtime High. Getting the children to church is like drawing teeth — urgent (never enough time in the morning), painful and occasionally bloody. But the atmosphere in the car on the way home is often merry and joyous; we ask the children what the readings were about and are often awed by the accuracy of the answers we get; we have a sense of a job well done, it is true, but we have also acquired new strength and resolutions for the week ahead.

The positive effect of spending just an hour thinking about God is remarkable, but it has taken us a long time to get to this point. If you are new to churchgoing with your children, be prepared to feel bruised and dispirited for a while, but be sure that things will get better.

Let teenagers make their own choices

If the world we live in believes that children and church do not mix, this is as nothing compared with the unshakeable belief that teenagers don't want to go to church. As one dad put it, 'Who else has to get up promptly on a Sunday morning, dress decently and spend much of the morning in a large dark room with grown-ups?' There cannot be an adolescent in the land who would not regard it as their virtual duty to refuse to go to church, if this was what their parents wanted of them.

On the other hand, adolescents have a powerful need to belong to a peer group and to make their own decisions within a strong family framework. From the age of about twelve, they need to be allowed to choose which service they want to go to, even to sit apart from the rest of the family if they so choose. If there is a good youth programme at your church, with young people's needs taken note of and respected, then you may find that your child stays with church for a bit longer.

At the same time, your child begins questioning the faith in new ways, challenging assumptions he or she has held since childhood. One mother said:

> We started having profound conversations about why we go to church, mainly because my daughter was not keen to come with us! It all turned out to be very useful and we cleared our own minds as well as hers.

It is at this age when the idea of a personal faith comes into conflict with the idea of belonging to a group faith. It is very easy to let a teenager off the hook of group faith because of his or her desire to be an individual, to be different, to be special and above all to be private. Yet faith, in whatever guise, is a group activity. It is of very little use carried out entirely in isolation. Without the strength of groups of people banding together, faith cannot be the spur of good works, of the building of hospitals, schools, the care of the starving and the homeless – all these good works which people of faith have made their own responsibility over the centuries.

You cannot force a great lumpish teenager to go to church, but you can look for easier alternatives for them. Many churches have youth activities and young people's groups; there may also be 'good works' that your young people are ready to help with, such as soup runs for homeless people. Few things work so effectively as a deterrent to teenage self-pity as proximity to the genuinely disadvantaged.

Let teenagers go church-tasting rather than let them sit at home watching Sunday morning television. Brian and Andrea have four children aged from seventeen down to seven and the older teenagers regularly peel off to their 'own' churches, travelling by bike or bus. At the last count, the family was patronising three different churches every Sunday. 'It's a bit complicated sometimes, but they get a lot out of feeling independent of us,' says Andrea.

Once you start looking for Christian youth-oriented stuff, it is surprising how much there is out there. There are a lot of perfectly street-credible rock performers who seem quite happy to be identified as Christians – few of these are home-grown British bands, but even your most sulky teen would agree that performers such as Moby and Lifehouse are not entirely lacking in cool. And as for Gospel music … well, where would the history of popular music be without it?

Ring the changes and look for different ways of worshipping

besides just going to church. Ask your minister/priest about pilgrimages, retreats, trips or expeditions that your teenager can join without having to be towed along by a parent. That such trips are connected with the church, by the way, is no guarantee of good behaviour – you will still have to be as vigilant as ever!

Just do it

Going to church with your family can be the most spiritually intoxicating experience of your life. It can lift a soggy, damp British weekend into something special. It can make you feel you can change the world. I rarely leave church without some degree of the Sunday Lunchtime High coursing through my veins. 'Where two or three are gathered in my name,' said Jesus, 'there am I with them.' This is the idea that started it all, so make the most of it.

'... daring to be different ...'

10

'We Don't Talk About It'

Being a Christian parent can be a very lonely business. You would never guess that 71 per cent of people in Britain consider themselves to be Christians, according to their census forms. Go to an average weekend barbecue, drinks party,

Daring to be Different

sports club social or dinner-party almost any-where in the United Kingdom – anywhere where professional middle-lifers are getting together to talk about their children's schools, the value of their homes and the rising tide of crime – and tell the person you are chatting with that you are a Christian. Then watch them melt away, leaving you standing on your own, staring into your drink.

'It's not something I discuss in public,' says Charlotte, a Christian mother of three daughters who runs a hospital trust. 'I expect as a matter of course to be the only believing Christian in a room, either at a social gathering or at any kind of professional meeting to do with my work.'

A million people a week attend Church of England services and another million attend Catholic services, and up to a million more attend services at churches of other denomina-tions. That amazing 2001 census figure of 71 per cent of the population who consider themselves Christians and millions more who adhere to other faiths stands for all to see. Yet a Christian at a party feels alone and out of place.

At the same time it is taken for granted that a safe cushion of belief exists, with a fully-functioning infrastructure, always there to be tapped into when wanted. When war with Iraq seemed imminent in early 2003 one of the Government's preparatory moves was to put the Church of England on a 'war footing' in readiness to cope with an unexpected flood of bereaved families. People who never set foot inside a church and who never give any kind of support to any church nonetheless expect it always to be there when they need it, ready to send in a crack division of rapid response vicars when the balloon goes up.

A Christian mother who feels odd and singular in society will naturally find it very hard to pass her faith on to her children with confidence. Her faith will start to falter.

Believing is hard work. The scariest part of being a family with faith is the way in which children challenge their parents' faith with awkward questions: usually, in my experience, in the car while you are trying to execute a U-turn in the middle of heavy traffic. Questions such as like 'Do people go to heaven if they don't believe in Jesus?' 'If Christians are meant to be good then how come they used to burn people at the stake?' 'How do you know that God is really there?' 'Why does God make bad things happen?' can fly out from the back of the car, hitting you in the back of the head, and may knock your faith off its perch for a while. If you are experiencing one of those grey days when the effort of belief is just too much, it is tempting to turn around (traffic conditions permitting) and say, 'Hell, I don't know the answer to your question. Probably because there isn't really an answer. Because the whole thing is just ridiculous. Let's give up believing in all this superstitious rubbish and be normal.' In other words, let's rejoin the majority – all 29 per cent of them.

The obvious first step towards dealing with this loneliness is to join a church, of course; but even that can be dispiriting if you fail to 'click' with local parishioners. They may all be much older than you, and unless you are prepared to get involved, you will find that a shy smile and a nod once a week is an extremely slow way of building up a friendship.

A few days spent on some kind of organised holiday or retreat which brings your family together with other faith families is a faster, more efficient way of building those bonds. A sense of community feeling builds up very quickly: we all know we are in the same boat, as the crazy, primitive Christians who are scorned by the outside world. We come together for a week or so to compare wounds and laugh about our hardships and then we go home revived, thinking, 'Hey! There are normal, sensible Christians out there, just like me!'

Treading on Snakes

This kind of group experience is tremendously valuable in counteracting the sense of embattlement which many people of faith feel. As an example, I recently found myself sitting amid the stucco pillars of the Royal Society of Literature near Buckingham Palace as one of an audience listening respectfully to author Philip Pullman, whose fiercely anti-Christian three-volume children's novel *His Dark Materials* is now a major feature film and a National Theatre stage play; and media scientist Richard Dawkins. Both these highly educated men have taken the trouble to come all the way to London in order to fulminate against the stupidity of anyone who believes in God. It becomes clear in the course of the evening that Pullman and Dawkins both know very little of religion or the churches from first hand experience, and are still nursing a grudge against the Church for its treatment of Galileo.

Opening the newspapers, a new revelation of ancient – and even not so ancient – atrocities committed by the ordinands of some church or other seems to appear every week. In the streets of major cities, gangs of youths shout 'paedophile' threateningly at Catholic priests if they take the risk of walking out in clerical garb and few nuns dare wear full habits outdoors: the nun's habit, one former Sister told me, 'is a red rag to every pervert and exhibitionist travelling on the Underground'.

Religion is treated as fair game for a joke. Picking up the London listings section of the paper I find, under Clubbing, a listing for The Church, a nightclub in a deconsecrated church 'where Australians come to worship on Sundays', as the paper trills. Looking through school prospectuses for my daughter, I notice that one of the top London day schools is boasting proudly of its recent school production of *Once a Catholic*, a comedy in which convent schoolgirls desecrate a figure of the crucified Christ.

Meanwhile, quietly and almost completely unnoticed, throughout London, in the country and in the world, there are millions of Christian priests, religious and lay people of all denominations working to help the poor, the sick, the forgotten, the homeless. Why are the Samaritans called the Samaritans? Why are most hospitals called Saint Somebody's? Every night Christians are among those picking up from the pavement the least loved of human people, those who have given up all hope, giving them a square meal, some advice and some dignity. Christians are involved in caring for children orphaned by AIDS and left to die on streets of the world's cities, caring for the elderly and dying . . . the list goes on. Exactly the same may be said of any of the major world faiths: their public face is as much in their charitable works as in their worship.

Thirty or forty years ago it was quite normal and respectable to believe in God. Now it is actually frowned on by mainstream intellectuals, and consequently by the media. Being 'religious' is a negative quality, not a compliment. 'I hear you're quite religious,' a footballer was recently asked by an interviewer. 'I'm Christian, yeah,' he responded, 'but I wouldn't say I was religious.' Go figure, as they say.

Consequently, Christians feel shy of wearing their faith on their sleeve. Said a mother of a four-year-old:

> My little girl was at a totally secular nursery school last year
> and I played down Lent — I did not want her going into
> school talking about giving things up for Lent, everyone
> would have said, 'What are you talking about?' I don't want
> her feeling embarrassed and different.

The British have never liked outward shows of feeling at the
best of times. But if a small child dares not talk of Lent at her
nursery school, something is surely very wrong. How can
parents with beliefs hope to keep their children's faith alive in
such a world?

Teresa Crabtree, a highly successful faith teacher and mother
of eleven children, believes that with determination and prayer,
faith can not only be kept alive in hostile circumstances: it actually thrives. She says:

> There is a group in America which picks up snakes as a reli-
> gious practice because it says somewhere in the Bible you
> shall pick up snakes and no harm shall come to you. Not
> surprisingly, this group's activities are banned.
>
> I think what Christ is really saying in that passage is that
> Christians and people of faith can live in very dangerous
> environments, morally speaking, and survive. We can walk
> through the snakes; if we pray and do as God wants, we shall
> survive.

The passage Teresa refers to here is Luke 10:19: 'See, I have
given you authority to tread on snakes and scorpions and over
all the power of the enemy; and nothing will hurt you.'

The world is certainly very hostile to religion when the latter
rears its head and tries to assert itself. It is very confusing. There
is strong criticism of any political leader who allows his or her
religious feelings to colour their decisions; but on the other hand,
people who profess religious belief yet fail to live up to its standards, such as errant priests, are even more strongly despised. We
are damned if we live by our religion and damned if we do not.

Any mention of religion and science instantly assumes a confrontation of some kind. Religion is always 'against' science. Yet there are many scientists who are also believers, such as Russell Stannard, a scientist best known for a series of children's science books under the umbrella title of 'Ask Uncle Albert'. Stannard's books show that anyone can take enormous delight in the world and how it is made, exploring its workings more and more deeply, yet at the same time have a belief in a Creator. In one story, www.here-i-am (Templeton Press), a child is guided around a virtual universe by God via his computer screen. The child's name, Sam, and the title are clear references to the story of Samuel, the prophet who heard God's voice calling in the night, and the story is partly a lesson in praying.

Brian, a biochemist and a Christian, told me:

> It is far from my experience that all scientists are religious sceptics. In fact I sometimes feel that it is impossible to work in a field like mine and not believe in God – it is all so extraordinary.

Just because science and religion are popularly set up as in opposition to each other does not mean they really are.

Living the Faith

Living a genuinely Christian life requires a spirit of rebellion in a world where the rich, the cool, the hip and the tough get more attention and kudos than the poor, the drab, the dowdy and the frightened.

As one parent put it to me:

> If you walk past a beggar in the street and your children never, ever see you get your purse out, if you never regard the lonely, unattractive person as someone worthy of being invited into your own home, then your children get the message that you are someone who talks about Jesus but

does not live the faith. And I think that does turn kids off religion as they grow older.

Do you remember the Christian family I referred to earlier, who make a regular habit of inviting homeless people or anyone whom the mother characterises, with a grin, as 'a bit on the wacky side' in for meals? The mother explained this practice to me while sitting in her sunny suburban conservatory. 'Aren't you worried about inviting drug addicts, people with criminal records, alcoholics into your home, right alongside your teenage children?' I asked, looking round at the neat, ineffably comfortable middle-class surroundings. She replied:

> Well, we have never had a bad experience from offering friendship to lonely or dysfunctional people. There is nothing to be frightened of in extending friendship to people a bit different from yourself. This is a big lesson to be learned which Jesus was trying to teach us all the time: 'If you do this to the least of my brothers, then you do it to me . . .'

This family literally invites 'sinners' into their home, in direct imitation of Christ. We felt very inspired by this example one Christmas and invited a couple, Ben and Jackie, who were living in a homeless hostel, for dinner on Christmas Eve. They were not complete strangers: every morning on the way to work, my husband passed Ben as he sat at his regular begging post, and they had become good friends. Ben had had some mental health problems and serious depression. Jackie had a complex range of illnesses that seemed to put her in hospital regularly. They never seemed to have any luck.

We made careful arrangements in advance to collect the couple, I cooked a wonderful turkey, the children laid the table, lit candles and wrapped presents. But there was no sign of our guests; no reply from their mobile phone, no answer when we went round to the hostel to find them. By about 9.00 p.m. the children were ravenous, so we sat down and dolefully ate the turkey and roast potatoes, vegetables, cranberry sauce, gravy, Christmas pudding, dates . . .

At first we were worried – we knew Jackie had recently been seriously ill and feared the worst. But after Christmas, when we finally ran into Ben again, he shrugged the matter off: they had gone out, 'had a row', and (this was implied) simply forgotten about our invitation. My husband mused:

> I think this is God's way of making us realise that it isn't all that easy being good. I mean, there we were, thinking, 'Oh we are so good, inviting homeless people to dinner, what a doddle.' And it turned out to be much trickier than we thought it would. We have learned something here.

Witnessing

Sometimes the best way to deal with your child's anxieties about being 'different' from the rest of society is to summon up the courage to let your child discover faith by himself or herself. Teenage pride dictates that no idea put forward by a parent is cool, but anything the teenager has discovered for himself is cool.

Ram Gidoomal, for example, became a Christian completely on his own. As a young man, bright, ambitious and with an excellent business head on his shoulders, he was, in his own words, a 'high value' individual for his family, and the idea of him leaving their traditional Hindu faith was bound to be a difficult one for them to accept. It was a long time before he could break to them the news that he had been reading the Bible while an undergraduate and become what he terms very carefully a 'follower of Christ'. In the end, his family came to accept the news with great good grace, perhaps feeling, as many people do, that some faith is better than no faith. If Ram had tried to force his new faith on his family, however, they might never have been able to come to terms with it at all.

Rather than seeing you preaching your faith at street corners, I feel that as a parent your job is to let your growing child see you putting your faith into practice and see it working for the good of others and the world. The only truly effective 'witness', says Mary Crowley, an advisor on running liturgies for children, is 'to create a situation where other people look at us and think, 'I want some of whatever it is they have got'. (Or, as the lady in the restaurant in *When Harry Met Sally* says, 'I'll have what she's having!')

'Witnessing', Christ left us in no doubt, is part of being a Christian. It means essentially being a testimonial for the faith, in the hope that you will persuade others to join it. It can mean going round a neighbourhood knocking on doors asking people if they would like to talk about Jesus. The usual answer to this question is 'No'. The most valuable result of this practice that I can see is that sometimes a lonely, housebound person acquires someone to talk to, which is wonderful in itself.

Unfortunately, the call to witness is one of the areas where faith and modern society just don't get on together because our society lays great stress on tolerance – principally, tolerance of other people's views and beliefs. We also have a sometimes confusing set of ideas about cultural diversity. We are proud to live in a world that at least tries to believe that all faiths are equally valid. We therefore disapprove of anyone who tries to persuade others that their faith is the one to go for.

For adults, it is not difficult to cope with the idea that our religion is bound up with our background and who our parents are, and therefore has a 'truth' for us as valid as that of someone else's religion. However as soon as children get hold of it and begin worrying at it, it begins to look very shaky. If *that* religion is as good as *this* one, then why is *this* one claiming to be true? They cannot both be true. If they are, why don't we swap over and become Hindus next month, Moslems the month after . . .?

'Why not indeed?' the secular world would answer. 'Go ahead –

swap your religion with your clothes, it's all the same, it is all a matter of lifestyle choices.'

But faith is not a lifestyle choice. It is a decision to live your *whole* life in a certain way. 'Witnessing' can mean not merely *telling* other people how great your faith is, but it can also mean *being* a testimonial for Christianity: in other words, proving that the system works literally by living the faith. It can mean providing a testimonial in the way we provide a testimonial for a product we have used and liked, or a good reference for a valued former employee seeking work elsewhere.

Wishing Not to Be Happy, But to Be Good

Another issue of conflict is the stress our society places on success. Success almost always implies material wealth: being poor but honest is not an option any more, and the concept that taste is superior to expense has more or less gone for good. When young people are criticised for lacking 'idealism' what is often really meant is that they are more concerned with working hard for material success than with walking barefoot in the park.

So many parents urge their children to 'look after number one', that 'the worst crime they can commit is to get caught', that 'the system' exists purely to be manipulated. Families with faith, by contrast, feel an obligation to regard material success as much less important than being honest, kind, generous and true. To put it bluntly, they feel that it is better to do badly in an exam than to cheat and come top, yet their children see examples of cheats and liars doing well all around them. 'Parents continually say they want their children to be happy,' observed a pastor friend of mine. 'There may be more to be said, in the long run, for wanting their children to be *good*.'

Keep an eye out for news stories of people of faith who can show that there are other goals worth striving for besides material success. Keep newspaper cuttings about any person acting in a brave and selfless way; stories about, or interviews with aid workers, doctors and priests that give some hint of the fulfilment of their work. If children can see stories of people who dare to be different, they will feel encouraged.

Religion Causes Conflict ...

'How can you justify Christianity when religion causes so much unhappiness in the world?' must be the most common question which families of faith have to put up with. It is a good question, and one we should welcome.

The answer to it is: 'If you look at what Jesus asked us to do, and look at the people who actually do live their lives by his words, then you will see the point of it all.' The people who cause trouble are invariably those who, sometimes wilfully, skew the Gospels to fit their own political or social ends; these are people who create a Jesus of their own making – fitting Jesus to suit their lifestyle choices, in other words. The problem is not with those who genuinely live according to their faith, but those who use their faith as a weapon against others. They are not those whose lives are worth copying; they do not elicit the 'I'll have what they've got' response.

A Family of Two Halves

What if one of you is committed to a faith, and the other is not? It is a very common situation among Christian families and I have been constantly surprised by how well many couples cope with having differing levels of belief. One mother of two said:

> My husband was received into the church just before we were married. Then the priest who received him, who was quite a charismatic character, died – and somehow, after that, my husband gave up the idea quickly. He remains silent when the subject of religion comes up.

I was very upset when he stopped practising, I must admit. But then I remembered how as a girl I had been surrounded by my family's very strong, unquestioning faith and I never lapsed at all, not even as a student. So when I got to university it was a big shock to be out in the world where 99 per cent of the people don't believe what I believe.

In this world there is some point in your life when you have to hit the fact that most people you are likely to run into don't share your beliefs. That is the 'picking up snakes' moment – the moment when your child, raised in your faith, has to come to terms with the idea of being a minority.

So for their two children, their father's inhibitions about embracing faith are just an early lesson in the way of the world: their mother feels that they are bound to come across people who don't share her faith at some point and might as well experience it within their own family. The family becomes a microcosm of the world outside.

Another issue on which faith families find themselves out on a limb is that of forgiveness. Some time ago child murderer Myra Hindley died in custody despite a long-running campaign for her release spearheaded by the Catholic peer, Frank Longford. Longford believed, after years of conversations with Hindley, that she was genuinely and totally repentant and as a Christian he believed she had earned mercy. (Far from being the gullible aristocrat his opponents painted him as, Longford was an experienced prison visitor.) The headline 'May She Rot in Hell' appeared on the front pages of Britain's tabloid newspapers. How should we explain this to our children? Mary Crowley remembers:

This was a teachable moment, a classic moment when Christians find themselves in conflict with public attitudes. As Christians we should not be hoping this woman rots in hell but praying for her soul – and we need to get this across to our children.

It was indeed a deeply uncomfortable moment for many parents: it would be so easy to join the mob mentality and hound down child murderers with the rest. But to do so is to turn our backs on the crucial Christian concept of repentance, a concept without which the faith loses its sense of hope.

★ ★ ★

Part of the joy of being a family with faith is the hunt for these 'teachable moments', moments when your faith jumps into the foreground and becomes relevant and interesting instead of being a dull Sunday-only affair. To be a family of faith you need some bravery, a sense of humour, a good dollop of persistence and – above all – a heart that is open to the possibility that a greater love than human love exists. If you have these, then you are ready to embark on the most exciting adventure of family life yet.

ALTERNATIVES for Simple Living
5312 Morningside Ave
P.O. Box 2787
Sioux City
Iowa 51106
website: www.simpleliving.org

Resources

CPW (Catholic People's Weeks)
c/o Ted Monks
89 Marlborough Park Avenue
Sidcup
Kent
DA15 9DY

Crusaders Holidays
Smithfield House
Crescent Road
Luton
LU2 0AH
tel. 01582 589842
website: www.crusaders.org.uk

Family Caring Trust
8 Ashtree Enterprise Park
Newry
Co. Down
BT34 1BY
tel: 028 3026 4174
website: www.familycaring.co.uk

MasterSun/MasterSki
Thames House
63-67 Kingston Road
New Malden
Surrey
KT3 3PB
tel: 020 8942 9442
website: www.mastersun.co.uk/

Wintershall Estate
Bramley
Nr Guildford
Surrey
GU5 0LR
tel: 01483 892167
website: www.wintershall-estate.com

The Woodland Trust
Autumn Park
Grantham
Lincolnshire
NG31 6LL
tel: 01476 581111
website: www.woodland-trust.org.uk